AMPUTEE IDENTITY DISORDER:
INFORMATION, QUESTIONS, ANSWERS, AND RECOMMENDATIONS ABOUT SELF-DEMAND AMPUTATION

by

Gregg M. Furth, Ph.D. &

Robert Smith, ChM, FRCSEd.

Foreword by Elisabeth Kübler-Ross, M.D.

© 2000, 2002 by Gregg M. Furth, Ph.D. &
Robert Smith, ChM, FRCSEd.

All rights reserved.
No part of this book may be reproduced, stored in a retrieval system, or transmitted by any means, electronic, mechanical, photocopying, recording, or otherwise, without written permission from the author.

Published By:
1stBooks
http://www.1stbooks.com

ISBN: 1-5882-0390-5

1stbooks rev. 5/15/02

For more information: AmputeeIdentity@Aol.com

Cover design is a compilation of asymmetrical and symmetrical mandalas including a human cell as a mandala. Special thanks to Bailey Cunningham whose consultation assisted with the book cover design. Her expertise from The Mandala Project is greatly appreciated. (http://www.mandala project.org)

ABSTRACT
AMPUTEE IDENTITY DISORDER: INFORMATION, QUESTIONS, ANSWERS, AND RECOMMENDATIONS ABOUT SELF-DEMAND AMPUTATION

by
Gregg M. Furth, Ph.D. &
Robert Smith, ChM, FRCSEd.

This study brings recognition to and broadens the scope of understanding that surrounds the syndrome of self-demand amputation of a healthy limb or digit, known as apotemnophilia[1,2]. Related literature on scarring, self-mutilation, transgendered surgery, and Internet support systems is reviewed. An etiology of this syndrome is examined through the writings of Freud and Jung. Case studies illustrating the existence of this syndrome are presented, along with 28 frequently asked questions, with answers, about apotemnophilia. Recommend-

---

[1] Apotemnophilia was the name originally given to this syndrome by Money, J., Jobaris, R. & Furth, G. (1977), in their article Apotemnophilia: Two cases of self-demand amputation as a paraphilia, in The Journal of Sex Research, 13 (2), 115-125. The name needs updating. It is awkward and inappropriate for the set of symptoms that define the syndrome. Professionals are presently working to determine a more accurate name, hopefully with subdivisions specifying the types of "needed" body changes which would give individuals their identity as they see themselves to be. However, for the purposes of this writing we remain using the older clinical terminology until the time when the name change is agreed upon and official.

[2] A previous edition of this book referred to the syndrome of self-demand amputation as Apotemnophilia, and this term was included in the title of that edition. In this edition the term Amputee Identity Disorder is used to refer to the syndrome, although its formal acceptance awaits approval by appropriate committees. Whereas the title of this new edition has been changed to reflect the new designation, the text remains identical to the first edition.

ations are given, along with a suggested differential diagnosis for a future Diagnostic and Statistical Manual (DSM –V).

TABLE OF CONTENTS

ABSTRACT iii
FOREWORD xi
CHAPTER I 1
INTRODUCTION 1
CHAPTER II 5
REVIEW AND DISCISSION OF RELATED
   LITERATURE 5
   Background 5
   Relation to Transgendered 7
   Support and Encouragement 11
   Sexual Component 13
   Freud: Aggressive and Destructive Instincts 14
   Jung's Insights 19
   Self-mutilating Behavior 28
   Relatedness 36
CHAPTER III 41
CASE STUDIES 41
   Case 2 43
   Case 3 44
   Case 4 45
   Case 5 46
   Case 6 46
CHAPTER IV 49
QUESTIONS AND ANSWERS 49
   1. What is apotemnophilia? 49
   2. What is a wannabe? 50
   3. What is a devotee? 50
   4. What is a pretender? 50
   5. What are wannabes on the internet sharing? 51
   6. Are the wannabes, devotees, or pretenders
      dangerous? 63
   7. How long has this syndrome been around? . 64
   8. When does the syndrome begin? 65

9. What is the most difficult part of this syndrome? 65
10. Is this syndrome hereditary or learned? 67
11. Is this syndrome oriented mostly toward men? 67
12. Is this syndrome dominated by a sexual orientation? 67
13. Is apotemnophilia a fetish? 68
14. Can an individual control this urge? 68
15. Does therapy help? 69
16. Is there medicine that can help this syndrome? 69
17. Why is it so difficult to have surgery carried out? 70
18. Does surgery help? 71
19. Which limb is usually involved? 73
20. Is there a specific site for amputation? 73
21. What can a person do about this syndrome? 74
22. Where can one who has this need seek support? 74
23. What do non-elective amputees think of this syndrome? 75
24. How do spouses and partners deal with this syndrome? 77
25. Does publicity help or hurt the apotemnophiliacs' case? 77
26. Is acrotomophilia the same as apotemnophilia? 79
27. What is mutilation, and how is it related? .. 81
28. Are therapists ready for this syndrome? 82

CHAPTER V 85

FUTURE RECOMMENDATIONS 85

REFERENCES 91

*"If you bring forth
what is within you,
what you bring forth
will save you.*

*If you do not
bring forth
what is within you,
what you do not
bring forth
will destroy you."*

*Gospel of St. Thomas
Gnostic Gospels*

FOREWORD

I have been dealing with death and dying for close to 50 years, trying to help people live fully until they die. This book brings to our awareness how this taboo topic of Apotemnophilia devours individuals and shows how their lives are endangered. We are beginning to understand that apotemnophiles die because of the lack of medical care necessary to help them live completely. Appropriate help must be assessed and aid needs to be provided to apotemnophiles from the helping professions through psychotherapy, behavioral therapy, medication, and in cases where it is deemed necessary, even surgery.

My path has taken me into taboo arenas, where death was not mentioned because it was a forbidden topic, when medical schools did not teach nurses and doctors how to work to help people live until they die their own natural deaths. Naturally, it does not surprise me and I would even expect that one of my students, Gregg Furth, would venture not only to the edge of a taboo topic, but also very much into the depths of it. C.G. Jung walked into the unconscious, and did not learn psychology from textbooks, but instead through life experience. Gregg too, dared to walk to the brink of this unconscious content and does not know it only academically. Robert Smith, as a surgeon, comes to this syndrome with great compassion and understanding, as I would hope more health care providers would. He has done exceptional work as a medical professional, daring to help by venturing into a taboo procedure to save lives.

It is obvious that Apotemnophilia is not a Body Dysmorphic Disorder and needs to be categorized in the future DSM-V as a syndrome unto itself. Furth and Smith present to us an introduction to this centuries old phenomenon and we need to bring more awareness and aid to the people who are in need. The need is for more support systems from professionals and lay individuals and families as well in order to break this wall of silence.

In all my decades of being a psychiatrist I have never dealt with or known of a single case or request for a surgical amputation. Although I had many, many cases of mutilation I cannot remember getting any training in the treatment of those cases. Reading this book helped me to understand some of the origins and complexities of apotemnophilia. I was saddened to hear of the deaths of those who suffer from this syndrome, from the consequences of amputation which could have been prevented. If more people would understand the pathology of the syndrome and not judge and dismiss it as a sick perversion, jumping to conclusions without understanding what they are dealing with, then the consequences of self-destruction and inadequate amputation could prevent individuals from dying.

I congratulate Furth and Smith for having the courage to bring this previously unknown and unstudied subject into the open and hopefully include this topic in the training of physicians and nurses in the 21st century.

Mazel tov,

Elisabeth Kübler-Ross, M.D.

CHAPTER I
INTRODUCTION

The purpose of this writing is to bring recognition to, and broaden the scope of understanding that surrounds the little-known syndrome of self-demand amputation of a healthy limb or digit, currently known as apotemnophilia. This syndrome was named in a 1977 article, "Apotemnophilia: Two cases of Self-Demand Amputation as a Paraphilia," by J. Money, R. Jobaris and G. Furth. At that time, with "the threat of malpractice charges, [it] was unlikely that there would be an early answer to the question of whether self-demand amputation is an effective form of therapy in apotemnophilia or not" (p. 125). The article proposed that "the answer will have to come from patients who have engineered an amputation for themselves and then are generous enough to volunteer themselves for post-surgical study" (p. 125). Twenty-three years later, we have post-surgical results, both from patients who have engineered an amputation and from patients who have undergone surgical amputation from a cooperating hospital and surgeon.

Related literature, limited as it is, is discussed in Chapter II. With the advancement of the Internet, individuals affected by this syndrome can more easily connect with others and share their dilemma. They can gain up-to-date information on developments in this little-known area of amputation desire. The sense of "aloneness" felt when carrying this desire can terrorize an individual. This solitary, desolate feeling is demoralizing. Two persons stated, via the Internet:

> the most painful part of all of this for me growing up was that I believed I was alone. I thought I must be the most bizarre person on the face of the planet to have these feelings…and I took the fact that there were no books on it to mean that I was alone.

> I'm feeling a little lost and am not sure what to say...because I recently discovered I'm a wannabe. I'm a nice, normal, highly functioning woman, who thought for the longest time that there was something horribly wrong with me—until I learned that there is a name for what I feel. I know I'm not "sick," and don't really feel guilty about it, but life is getting a little intolerable knowing this about myself, but not really understanding it. I don't know who else to talk to, and certainly don't want counseling. I'm hoping a list like this might help [referring to a list that is being made up to give to the medical profession, asking for surgery assistance].
> Internet:www.angelfire.com/or/want2be/
> (November 15, 1999)

This writing brings this subject into the public arena to help those living with this desire to realize that they are not alone. Support systems are available via the Internet. Literature is slowly becoming available through research. The syndrome is being recognized, and both therapy and surgery have been achieved, helping people with varying degrees of success. More importantly, this writing can inform and educate the medical professionals who do not know about this syndrome. This education and awareness will bring hope to clients, so that they do not have to jeopardize their lives, or even die, because they are "swallowed by this desire." If individuals choose to remain private and unknown to the world, the Internet, with related literature, is available to them, as well as references given in this book. Privacy can be maintained.

Brief pre- and post-surgical case studies illustrating the need for acknowledgment of the validity, reliability and seriousness concerning the existence of this philia are in Chapter III. These cases give more understanding to the syndrome. The patients' reported histories came from records that included letters, tape recordings, personal interviews, telephone calls, public information records, newspaper articles and data from psychiatric interviews and evaluations. Identifying information has been changed and altered to protect client confidentiality.

Chapter IV contains frequently asked questions and answers to further the understanding of this syndrome. The reader is cautioned that the answers are those of the authors, obtained from their experience with patients, readings, and suggestions from those "saddled" with this desire. No assumption is made that these are right and correct answers for everyone. Readers should assume that everyone is unique and individual.

Everaerd (1983) reports that this unheard-of condition was documented more than a century ago. There is still much controversy about comprehension, understanding, and treatment of this condition. Chapter V contains recommendations for research, study, and development.

To enter into this world, daring to comprehend what this philia is about, the reader must agree to a few premises:

1.) understand that everyone has his or her individual psychology, and that others do not necessarily have the same psychology as the reader,
2.) dare to set aside personal prejudices; endeavor to be open, be willing to listen to another's reality, regardless of how it may differ from one's own, and
3.) understand that the primary goal is for respect, that this syndrome is a real-life occurrence for many individuals, and that they suffer from it.

If the reader can agree to these three premises, progress may be made for all concerned. Consciousness, education, acceptance, understanding, respect, and cordiality are needed.

CHAPTER II
REVIEW AND DISCISSION OF RELATED LITERATURE

Background

Body Dysmorphic Disorder, formerly Dysmorphophobia (DSM-IV, 1994, p. 466), is one description that some psychotherapists use to label individuals convinced of a defect in their physical appearance. **THIS IS AN INCORRECT DIAGNOSIS.** Apotemnophiles do **not** believe they have a defect in the limb or digit, for which they desire amputation. They are persons who need to have one or more healthy limbs or digits amputated to fit the way they see themselves. They want to rid themselves of a limb that they believe does not belong to their body identity. Other terms used to describe the syndrome and the apotemnophiliac are amelotasis, dysmorphic, elective amputee, and voluntary or self-demand amputee. Some of these individuals also are acrotomophiliacs (see Chapter IV).

Most apotemnophiliacs do not want amputation in order to become disabled. Rather, they see themselves with an amputated limb as becoming able-bodied and more fully functioning, more whole, more complete. They suffer extreme distress over their body being intact, with feelings of torment and an overpowering desire to realize the physical image which corresponds to their self perception. They often feel driven to obtain the amputee image. Frequently, development of the desire originates in early childhood, becoming fully manifest in consciousness by puberty. At first, most clients report that they tried to rid themselves of the desire, but eventually they could not resist its power. To become more whole as a limbless person dominates these individuals' psyches, and this sovereignty leads many apotemnophiliacs, if not all, to contemplate self-inflicted injury to hasten and necessitate amputation by medical professionals. Fortunately, many who suffer resist this impulse and suppress the urge. Some seek support from other "wannabes" (see Chapter IV). A few disclose their secret desire to best friends, partners, or spouses, hoping for support. Others attempt therapy, be it analytical psychology, psychoanalysis, behavioral therapy, or even drug therapy. The research shows that suppressing the urge is temporary. The compulsion builds until the individuals are again preoccupied with thoughts and fantasies of the initial desire.

What is extraordinarily interesting to notice about this heightened feeling when apotemnophiliacs report their desire to friends, spouses, or partners, is that they often receive affirmation and acceptance. Just as many people understand the need of transsexuals for a body with which they can more naturally identify, many people likewise understand the apotemnophilacs' situation, and are more accepting than expected.

The closest related literature to this syndrome concerns the experience of the transsexual. Explaining apotemnophilia from this vantage point helps people comprehend what apotemnophiliacs desire. Often, apotemnophiliacs are surprised to be so understood and supported. They have spent so many years questioning and wrestling with this, this need. To most wannabes who have told their therapists of this desire, their therapists responded with, "never heard of such a desire," or, "you'll grow out of it," or "we won't deal with that, as you will see, it'll go away on its own." When we hear that psychologists, psychiatrists, and analysts respond in this inappropriate way, it tells us that these professionals need education (see question #28). It is also necessary to educate apotemnophiliacs that it can be helpful for them to tell not only their therapists, but also their family and close friends. If the public can comprehend that what apotemnophiliacs want is comparable to what transsexuals want, then this is a good approach for those seeking an explanation. Hopefully, more research will be forthcoming to establish the etiology of this phenomenon, perhaps promoting a better understanding, thus making educating others easier.

This amputation need is most closely related to the transforming element of the transgendered. Similarly, individuals who seek and do mutilation: body piercing, scarring, body cutting, tattoos, nail biting, trichotillomania, or are anorexic, bulimic, smokers, or are obese, fall under the category of altering their healthy body form. Similarities are obsessive-compulsive manifestations, such as frequent mirror checking or imaging of what one could look like if one were one-legged, thinner, scarred, longer-nailed, with or without hair, or tattooed. According to the Diagnostic and Statistical Manual of Mental Disorders (1994), cited throughout this writing as the DSM-IV, "body dysmorphic disorders may be more common than was previously thought" (p. 467). On this basis, apotemnophiles, most likely, are not a small number of affected individuals. Statistically, it could range between one to three percent of the population. We know that many people often wish for different body features: hoping for longer legs, thinner thighs, higher cheekbones, a smaller waist, larger biceps, larger breasts, or a change in genitalia. It is natural for this feeling to be present, but in some cases an obsession/compulsion sets in, and individuals develop extreme demands, such as apotemnophilia.

Relation to Transgendered

Because the desire for body change is prevalent and normal, most people can comprehend the apotemnophiliac's position, as so many in our culture and society understand the transgendered. Many people in our society are fascinated by "the other." Whether "the other" is the amputee, the obese one, the bald woman or man, the anorexic, or the one who stutters, it does not matter. When someone walks down the street on crutches, or is in a wheelchair, or is an obese person trying to sit in a chair that may not provide support, people stare. Whether it is done out of pity, admiration, or desire—people see "the other." Fascination in "the other" exists. To admit to this fascination can be embarrassing, humiliating, and even shameful. Nevertheless, the intrigue, to some extent, exists in all of us. The fascination is so prevalent that the Chicago Group, comprised of amputees and members who are devotees interested in meeting amputees, named itself *Fascination*. As stated earlier, apotemnophilia is more prevalent than expected. It is not a body dysmorphic disorder as some psychotherapists have diagnosed it from the

DSM-IV (1994). It is a syndrome unto itself, which unfortunately the DSM-IV (1994) has not as yet categorized. (See Chapter V for a recommended categorization write-up of this syndrome suggested for the forthcoming DSM-V.)

It is more important to discover how to explain the existence and development of this desire. Dr. Sheila Kirk (1995), board certified in Obstetrics and Gynecology and a member of the Harry Benjamin International Gender Dysphoria Association, writes in The TV/TS Tapestry journal, that there are, to date, "no answers to why transgendered exist. There are no answers to the questions of accurate and appropriate diagnosis, nor to the good psychological and medical therapies" (p. 9). Similarly for apotemnophiliacs there are, as yet, few answers for the many questions about the desire. As to the etiology of apotemnophilia, I found only Freud and Jung contributing some insight (see Chapter II). Professionals are just beginning to hear of this syndrome. The future will tell if professionals pay heed and see its relationship to individual clients, as well as to its impact on our society. Dr. Kirk writes, "rare diseases and syndromes engender more interest" (p. 9), so she claims that transgenderism is passed by because it "is not rare and is not a disease entity" (p. 9). I do not know how she comes to her assessment of transgenderism, but I see apotemnophilia as a syndrome that is rare when it goes to the extreme of self-demand amputation of a healthy limb. I would assume it is rare and extreme to opt for transgender surgery. She admits that most medical professionals are "turned off" by transsexuals and surgeons are usually not interested. It is the same for the apotemnophiliac. Some doctors automatically reject the request of the individual wanting surgery without even asking or seeking further information. They can be rigid, or think they know what is best for the patient. What they do not know is that they do not know.

Dr. Kirk (1995) offers advice to the transgender community that the apotemnophiliac community should heed. She says, "It boils down to education and money" (p. 10). The education and finances for enlightening our society about apotemnophilia must begin with the community of the wannabes, pretenders, and devotees (see Chapter IV). The shame, disgrace, embarrassment, morality, ethical issues, and taboos must be acknowledged and dealt with. If apotemnophiliacs cannot come forward with their inmost desires, how can our society learn what this syndrome is about, let alone be supportive in any constructive way? Courage is needed, education is demanded, and then enlightenment and change may follow.

The media—radio, newspapers, magazines, television, and the Internet enjoy this topic because it is sensationalistic. Sensationalism sells, especially if photographs are included. Few journalists seem to care about the individuals whom they write about. The British Broadcasting Corporation (BBC) in London has made the only documentary on the topic, thus far, and its female producer/director has seriously studied and filmed a documentary on the transgendered. Consequently, she is exceptionally empathetic to the syndromes of the transsexual and the apotemnophiliac. Her research assistant originally discovered the subject matter of elective amputation. He is an amputee and heard of wannabes and devotees suffering and dealing with the desire for loss, similar to his actual limb loss. He reported that the feelings and words were the same in the opposite situation, that the apotemnophiliac suffers having an unwanted limb. He became interested not just academically, but with empathy from his personal experience and understanding of what was being revealed. Their documentary approach and methodology should be emulated.

Medical schools and the medical profession need to grow in understanding. There are several very helpful psychiatrists and psychologists, and a few surgeons who comprehend the issues involved and are willing to assist with education, and where necessary, agree that some apotemnophiles are good candidates for actual amputation, as a last resort, after comprehensive assessment, when all other remedies have failed.

These professionals realize that the apotemnophiliac more than likely cannot move into the symbolic understanding and are caught in enacting the image. The energy of the image can lead some individuals to endangering their lives in an attempt to acquire the body form they desire and a consequence is that some of these individuals die from this enactment. In these circumstances, surgery may prevent greater harm to the client and provide psychic relief.

We have come to accept that a sex-change operation does not violate the Hippocratic oath's command: First, "do no harm." The operation violates the physical integrity of healthy sex organs to relieve the psychic pain from being born in the wrong body. The difficulty many will perceive in the removal of healthy limbs to relieve the apotemnophiliac's psychic pain is that the final status of being an amputee does not receive the positive endorsement of the final status which a transgendered person achieves by an operation. Being male or being female is regarded as a positive outcome. Being an amputee is not regarded as a favorable outcome. It is only better than being dead, not better than having healthy limbs.

Perhaps a saying of Jesus may be of some help.

> ... if your hand causes you to stumble, cut it off. It is better for you to enter life maimed than to have two hands and go to hell, to the unquenchable fire. And if your foot causes you to stumble, cut it off. It is better for you to enter life lame, than to have two feet and to be thrown into hell. And if your eye causes you to stumble, tear it out. It is better for you to enter the kingdom of God with one eye than to have two eyes and to be thrown into hell, where their worm never dies and the fire is never quenched. (Mark, 9:43-48, New Revised Standard Version)

The church has never favored a literalistic interpretation of these verses, but seeking to kill the worm and quench the fire which keeps people in psychic hell may allow them to enter life maimed, but be at peace psychically.

The reluctance to view amputation as a desirable treatment relates to an almost universal perception of amputation as undesirable, tragic, and dehumanizing, despite contrary evidence provided by many thousands of happy, well-adjusted, thoroughly-rehabilitated involuntary amputees. Non-objective views toward the "harm" of amputation perpetuate prejudice against the concept of viewing amputation as the best available choice. Amputation is always a choice, except in the case of direct, traumatic amputation. Even as a life-saving procedure, it is a choice requiring a value judgement. The choice of "elective" amputation in non-terminal cases becomes more difficult because of the wide variation in values assigned to amputation and its results by different individuals. When amputation is performed on an unhealthy, unsightly, or poorly functional but salvageable limb, a choice is made. Two cases with identical or similar defects may result in different choices and outcomes because of value judgements made by the individuals involved. The overwhelming tendency to dismiss amputation as an alternative to chronic psychic pain is a choice, traditionally made by individuals who have never felt that pain and who do not understand it. Amputation is a choice that would be gladly made by the apotemnophile, but it is denied by those who fail to acknowledge his pain and suffering.

Lastly, upon returning to the comparison of the transgendered and the apotemnophile we note that secrecy frequently surrounds both syndromes. Secrecy seems to be a common dominant problem in body augmentation. Kay Metsker (1989) states in her writing, "One of the major stumbling blocks towards self-acceptance for many transsexuals is their reluctance to share their problem with their parents" (p. 23). She recognizes that people keep the secret because they are protecting themselves from disapproval. Most likely these individuals are not secure, are limited in self-esteem, and fear rejection from others. This is further complicated because the inner rejection exists by keeping the fear. The apotemnophiliac may become more and more alone, and more and more desperate. Tragedies happen when desperation prevails.

Support and Encouragement

Support and encouragement must be given to help those with this desire to speak to therapists, to support groups, and to their loved ones. Metsker (1989) writes that, naturally, relationships that are "charged with emotional content" are the most difficult in which to be open and honest (p. 23). "We have the most to lose.... To alter the relationship...is frightening and threatening" (p. 23). She urges clarity in what one wants to convey; no blame, anger, or hostility; to think clearly what they want others to understand, and to work to convey that content.

Family and loved ones have rights to their feelings, so a support system helps the individual who is sharing to stand steady, and keeps reactions brief and options open. Metsker (1989) cites the Kubler-Ross' (1969) five stages of grief (denial, anger, bargaining, depression, and acceptance) that family members may need to pass through as they become conscious of what their loved one is explaining to them. These same ideas are constructive and valuable for apotemnophiliacs when speaking to their families and support systems. Individuals should remember that family and loved ones may not understand this desire for amputation and may need time to grieve the perceived loss. With time, their loved one can be seen in a new light and perhaps will be accepted.

Metsker (1989) ends her writing with this quote from Jung:

> Every one of us gladly turns away from his problems; if possible they may not be mentioned, or better still, their experience is denied. We wish to make our lives simple, certain, and smooth. For that reason problems are taboo. The artful denial of a problem will not produce conviction; on the contrary, a wider and higher consciousness is called for to give us the certainty and clarity we need. (p. 23)

Jung clearly states that secrecy does not help to solve the dilemmas. He indicates that "higher consciousness" helps us find answers to questions, such as, is this phenomenon sexual, biological, instinctual, or psychological?

Sexual Component

In <u>Transgendered Nation,</u> Gordene Olga MacKenzie (1994), writes, "audience response to ... a transsexual suggests that many people still believe that gender is inseparable from sex" (p. 117). Frequently, apotemnophilia is also aligned with a sexual component. This seems to be a biased perception. When the research dealing with the phenomenon of body dysmorphia was gathered in the late 1960s and early 1970s, it indicated that (1) some individuals were involved for the sexual gratification and (2) some were involved because they deemed it necessary to live life in a different body form. For the first category of individuals, the sexual component was very important, but for the second, what was significant was to be living life while being in a different body, namely the body of an amputee. The question arose as to who could be of help and relate to this request, bizarre as it seems, in order to comprehend and perhaps aid individuals who were suffering from this disorder. After all, surgery seemed to be what was desired and the closest physiological type to this diagnosis was the transsexual. The big difference is that transsexual surgery is to the genitalia instead of to a limb.

In group 1, the desire is part of sexual arousal and may either be a cause or result of such arousal. These individuals tend to have the desire only before or during sexual arousal and this desire fades after climax. The desire also tends to vary with regard to which limb, the number of limbs and the level of amputation required. In group 2, the desire is much more compelling and usually related to activities of daily living. It tends to be a constant desire and the individual always focuses on the same limb and level of amputation. Unlike group 1, the desire may or may not be also associated with sexual arousal and remains after sexual climax. Members of Group 1 are less likely to have a satisfactory outcome from surgery, as the desire is intermittent and variable. Group 2 has a constant desire related to their activities of daily living and should have a good result from surgery.

In the early 1970s John Money was doing extraordinary work on transsexual reassignment at Johns Hopkins Hospital in

Baltimore, Maryland. At that time, the original research on apotemnophilia was brought to him for his evaluation and to inquire if any surgery or therapy were available. His research team was not aware of this new information and this research. No known literature had been cited on the subject matter. Within a few years, more data was compiled which was published for the first time in "Apotemnophilia: Two cases of Self-Demand Amputation as a Paraphilia" (1977). The article, because it came from a clinic dealing with sex reassignment, was assumed to be dealing with this phenomenon as a sexual fetish. This misjudged those who felt in their soul, in their psyche, that they are uncomfortable in a body that has all its limbs. This desire is unrelated to sex. Apotemnophiliacs are not talking about rational thinking when they believe that they will be more comfortable in a limbless body. Rational thinking would have logos/logic and would be explainable. However, it is a non-rational way of thinking, which is real and alive to the person who feels it and carries it and, thus, it is unexplainable to themselves and to others (note that it is not stated as irrational, for the irrational is without reason). The apotemnophiliac is operating on the non-rational axis, and has a definite reason for the request to have a limb or digit amputated, because of the strong need and feeling from within.

Freud: Aggressive and Destructive Instincts

Freud (1964) did not write about apotemnophilia *per se*, but did write about the "impulsion to self-destruction" (1964, p. 105). He hypothesizes that the theory of the instincts is "based essentially on biological considerations" (p. 103). He sees two different classes of instincts: 1) the sexual instincts and 2) the aggressive instincts. Basically, the sexual instincts are classified as Eros (love, relatedness) and the aggressive instincts are classified as hate or destruction. It is the marriage of opposites: "loving and hating" (p. 103). This experience of the opposites is felt by many as something to avoid --"which should be got rid of as quickly as possible" (p. 103).

Freud (1964) ponders why human beings hesitate to recognize their inner aggressive instincts. His proposal is that we would expect and accept it in the animal world, yet we readily reject the syndrome in the "human constitution," as it might be

> sacrilegious; it contradicts too many religious presumptions and social conventions. No, man must be naturally good or at least good-natured. If he occasionally shows himself brutal, violent or cruel, these are only passing disturbances of his emotional life, for the most part provoked, or perhaps only consequences of the inexpedient social regulations which he has hitherto imposed on himself.
>
> Unfortunately, what history tells us and what we ourselves have experienced does not speak in this sense but rather justifies a judgment that belief in the 'goodness' of human nature is one of those evil illusions by which mankind expects their lives to be beautified and made easier while in reality they only cause damage. (p. 104)

Freud (1964) shows by "examining the phenomenon of sadism and masochism" (p. 104) that a unique aggressive and destructive instinct exists in the human being. By definition, sadism is sexual pleasure obtained from inflicting cruelty, pain and humiliation, and masochism is when receiving the inflicted cruelty, pain and humiliation, satisfies a need. Freud makes it very clear that these "two trends are included in normal sexual relations" (p. 104).

Freud states that sadism and masochism are excellent examples of the two classes of instinct, Eros and aggressiveness, and claims that they are a "model" (1964, p. 104). They illustrate the impulse that consists of a fusion of the two classes of instincts for existence. He points out that the fusions would vary in magnitude. This may answer why some individuals only scar themselves, or why some individuals want to be around an amputee as a devotee and do not want to be an amputee themselves. The instinctual degree of destruction is milder for one individual as compared to another, depending on this fusion of sadism and masochism. The Eros side of the balance to aggressiveness would introduce the varied sexual aims of desire and enactment. Therefore, there could easily be gradations of Eros in an individual, as well as gradations of aggressiveness. These gradations could vary in the level of active violation to oneself--ranging from nail biting to eating disorders, smoking abuse, alcohol abuse, scarring, and even to acts of mutilation, such as amputation of a limb or limbs; in other words, to the life of an apotemnophiliac.

Freud (1964) writes,

> This hypothesis opens a prospect to us of investigations which may some day be of great importance for the understanding of pathological processes. For fusions may also come apart, and we may expect that functioning will be most gravely affected by defusions of such a kind. But these conceptions are still too new; no one has yet tried to apply them in our work. (p. 105)

Perhaps for the apotemnophiliac, the fusions have separated. The enactment of masochistic tendency against oneself is monumental and often one sees little sadism being acted out. Perhaps this indicates that if apotemnophiliacs were more assertive and aggressive with others, the impulse within to self-destruct would be held in balance, and would not have to be acted upon. Furthermore, if one were to take the theory that Eros is on the opposite side of the scale to the natural human aggressive instinct, and one instinct overpowers the other, the scales are out of balance. To rebalance the scales, one would activate the instinct with lower libido by taking libido away from the overpowering instinct. What this means is, if apotemnophiliacs want to be aggressive toward themselves, and if this impulse is overriding and overpowering them, then, more than likely, there is little Eros in their lives at that time. The input of Eros would diminish the aggressive instinct.

This has been proven. Some pretenders have stated that when they tie themselves up and act as an amputee or disabled individual, they act out a sexual fantasy either with their partner or by themselves through masturbation. They report that once they climax, they are immediately ready and willing to untie themselves, having satisfied their libido. Similarly, some transvestites report dressing up and living out the pretender life, but upon climax they also are ready to take the clothing off and resolve never to do it again, even though it may happen again. The relatedness of Eros has balanced the aggressive instinct. This aggressiveness no longer owns the individual. Similarly, apotemnophiliacs may be overly involved in the aggressive instinct and short-changing themselves with regard to the eros instinct.

This aggressive instinct's aim is self-destruction. Freud writes that the aggressive destructive instinct is very natural and normal in life: "such ideas are not foreign even to physiology . . . the mucous membrane of the stomach digests itself" (1964, p. 106). The destruction of one's own body is definitely a taboo. This is why so many apotemnophiliacs who have damaged their bodies have wrestled with the moral and ethical issues associated with it. For some, the aggressive instinct overwhelmed the taboo and they enacted their plan. The taboo is important for the culture to retain because it helps, in most situations, to protect one from outright aggressiveness toward oneself.

But, being silent and pretending that one does not have this aggressive instinct, can be a problem for any member of society. Freud created a furor in the early 1900s which caused him to back off his stress on the aggressive instinct. He learned to remain quiet about its implications because of the negative reception he received and only years later did he take it up and continue to write on this topic. Today, almost 100 years later, the phenomenon of apotemnophilia similarly creates a furor or is passed over in silence, or treated with shame and guilt.

Not acknowledging or addressing this aggressive instinct is like a pressure cooker when the lid finally blows off. Children taking weapons to school, terrorizing, maiming, and killing their peers and teachers (such as at Columbine High School in Colorado in 1998) is an example of this. This aggressive nature must have its "right to life," but be balanced with Eros.

For the apotemnophiliac, the aggressive instinct is thwarted in its sadistic aspect and overcompensates in the masochistic dimension, thus the desire for amputation. For the school children attacking others, this imbalance is in reverse. The sadistic aspect is advanced and the masochistic dimension is undeveloped and misunderstood. Freud states "that we only perceive [the destructive instinct] under two conditions: if it is combined with erotic instincts into masochism or if--with a greater or lesser erotic addition--it is directed against the external world as aggressiveness" (1964, p. 105).

The problem is that aggressiveness is not able to come alive or find gratification in the outer world because culture and society usually disdain or forbid it. When this occurs, the energy of the destructive instinct swings back within the individual, increasing its self-destructive force with no safety valve. Freud (1964) states,

> Impeded aggressiveness seems to involve a grave injury. It really seems as though it is necessary for us to destroy some other thing or person in order not to destroy ourselves, in order to guard against the impulsion to self-destruction. A sad disclosure indeed for the moralist! (p. 105)

So, apotemnophilia may be attributed to the obstruction of the natural aggressive instinct. The goal of self-destruction is conscious (perhaps driven from the unconscious). Apotemnophiliacs have no training to constrain themselves from this "impulsion." The aim is to carry the natural destructive energy, constructively balanced with the eros instinct. Both instincts need to be incorporated into the life of the apotemnophiliac.

> So, in reality, Freud (1964) states, the need for punishment is the worst enemy of our therapeutic efforts. It is satisfied by the suffering which is linked to the neurosis, and for that reason holds fast to being ill. It seems that this factor, an unconscious need for punishment, has a share in every neurotic illness. And here those cases in which the neurotic suffering can be replaced by suffering of another kind are wholly convincing. (p. 108)

Freud postulates that the internalized need for punishment attached to aggressiveness could well be, for lack of better wording, "an unconscious sense of guilt." He sees it as being taken over by the super-ego, the part of the psyche that is the conscience, and moral, judgmental value system, that tells us what and what not to do, and what is accepted by our culture and not acceptable by our culture. A child would naturally have the aggressive instinct within as he/she grows and develops. However, for example, if the child is forbidden to express this aggressive instinct, its energy flows back into the child internally, and eventually demands expression. If it cannot go outward, it turns against itself, and a destructive force results in some activity--an accident-prone child, head banging, nail biting, or apotemnophilia. Fortunately, the aggressive instinct is never alone. It always has its opposite, i.e. Eros. The hope is that Eros and the aggressive instinct will counterbalance each other, so that they keep each other "in check."

Jung's Insights

> Jung, though not addressing apotemnophilia directly, gives us insight into this phenomenon when he writes on complexes, their energy and goal. Additionally, when applying his concepts to apotemnophilia, other questions are answered concerning its effect and outcome on the apotemnophiliac's life. Jung (1969) writes, "Everyone knows nowadays that people 'have

complexes.' What is not so well known, though far more important theoretically, is that complexes can have us" (p. 96). This is precisely the situation of wannabes (see Chapter IV, Question # 2). Frequently, apotemnophiliacs mention how overwhelming the image of the amputee is for them. This desire is so powerful that they cannot help or even control themselves. They plot to engineer accidents, such as drilling into their leg, throwing their limb under a passing train, using a shot-gun, a meat cleaver, or a guillotine to damage or dismember the undesired limb. These individuals all report the suction power of the feeling to become an amputee, aiming for the desired body image, as their ultimate goal.

Jung (1969)

indicates that the driving force is from the feeling-toned complex. It is the *image* of a certain psychic situation which is strongly accentuated emotionally and is, moreover, incompatible with the habitual attitude of consciousness. This image has a powerful inner coherence, it has its own wholeness and, in addition, a relatively high degree of autonomy, so that it is subject to the control of the conscious mind to only a limited extent, and therefore behaves like an animated foreign body in the sphere of consciousness. The complex can usually be suppressed with an effort of will, but not argued out of existence, and at the first suitable opportunity it reappears in all its original strength. ...its intensity or activity curve has a wavelike character, with a 'wave-length' of hours, days, or weeks. This very complicated question remains as yet unclarified. . . . as one might expect on theoretical grounds,

> these impish complexes are unteachable. (pp. 96-97)

Unteachable—what Jung indicates is that the complex or syndrome cannot be argued out of its power via thinking or logos. It has the power of desire behind it. Desire in itself carries the feeling tone to which Jung refers. The desire could, therefore, contain the answer as to why apotemnophiliacs want to be limbless. Human beings can only desire what they had in life at one time or another. In other words, the desire was taken away at some point and they want to return to it. One might wonder, but apotemnophiliacs want to be limbless and they never were missing a limb - that's the issue. We are not speaking consciously, we are speaking of what the unconscious wants. That's part of the confusion. At an unconscious level, the unconscious lives in symbols, and if this desire is connected with such grave feeling and can be seen as a feeling-tone complex or syndrome, it communicates itself through symbols. Jung (1969) writes,

> the unconscious contents want first of all to be seen clearly, which can only be done by giving them shape, and to be judged only when everything they have to say is tangibly present. . . .It does not suffice in all cases to elucidate only the conceptual context . . . it is necessary to clarify a vague content by giving it a visible form. (p. 86)

Apotemnophiliacs have given the desire a visible form and fantasize, even strive to seek back their status which, at one point in their life, was so "tasteful" and gratifying. To return to this experience of being desired, loved, wanted, and needed is the major goal. It is these feelings that apotemnophiliacs believe will be regained once they become an amputee. This is what is sought. The feeling of finding one's totality is invested onto the symbol, in this case, onto being an amputee. Thus, it could be, the amputee wannabe wants the limb removed, because it was removed symbolically earlier in life. They have a deep inner need to return to the original status. The desire to be an amputee is real, coming from the unconscious which speaks via symbols. Apotemnophiliacs react to the image, want to achieve this status, and are unconcerned about its deeper meaning.

Jung writes that not all psychologies can deal with unconscious content. It very well could be that not all apotemnophiles can work with the inner image as symbolic material which stems from the unconscious. In other words, some individuals may find themselves coming into wholeness by enacting the image of their desire and need. Yet other apotemnophiles can find their wholeness by working with the unconscious content of their desire by understanding and living with it on a symbolic level.

First, I need to define some terms. Jung (1971) writes,

> When I speak of image...I do not mean the psychic reflection of an external object, but a concept derived from poetic usage, namely, a figure of fancy or *fantasy-image,* which is related only indirectly to the perception of an external object. This image depends much more on unconscious fantasy activity, and as the product of such activity it appears more or less abruptly in consciousness, somewhat in the manner of a vision...but without possessing the morbid traits that are found in a clinical picture. The image has the psychological character of a fantasy idea.... (p.442)

An unconscious image which the apotemnophile first sees as a sign has only one meaning and one meaning only. It is simply a sign for this one point. An apotemnophile does not see this image as a symbol which could have as many meanings as there are people in this world, and more. A symbol is never ending, whereas a sign has one definite, unchangeable, agreed upon message to all people. For example, a stop sign regardless of where in the world you find it, will always have the consistent meaning, "stop." This is an example of a sign.

On the other hand, the moon as a symbol could mean love to one person, romance to a different person, a wish to yet another, and enlightenment to someone else. On a personal level it could have thousands of meanings, never ending. However, on a collective level, the symbol of the moon has a universal significance of being feminine, as the moon is on a monthly cycle similar to the feminine being on a monthly cycle. We could go on and on with more symbols, such as the sun, stars, trees, etc. which are indefinable as having one meaning, yet signs have one and only one meaning universally.

Some individuals can move to symbolic thinking, some remain outside of this and with time can perhaps find symbolic thinking. However, there are some psyches that do not want to enter into symbolic thinking and want to stay outside it, must stay outside it, and may even be unable to enter into this domain. This has no reflection on the quality of the psyche, whichever realm it exists within. We have to be open to psyches being where they are and being able to traverse, or not being able to traverse into symbolic work.

With this in mind, an illustration of Jungian theory and an example will be presented. When this is understood, let us hook our knowledge of theory with sign and symbol unto the apotemnophile's desire.

When deeply rooted syndromes of the unconscious are examined, violent resistances are provoked and it takes a lot of effort to overcome them. Jung explains that we can have four attitudes towards such a syndrome:

Stage 1. we can be unconscious of it, basically we deny its existence,

Stage 2. we identify with it,

Stage 3. we project it,

Stage 4. we can confront it.

Using alcoholism as an example, it could occur that when an alcoholic is confronted with a problem of drinking they might immediately deny its existence. They could even state, "I am not an alcoholic." This is stage one, denial of the syndrome.

A response from an inebriated person whose friends and colleagues confront him might be, "If you think I have a drinking problem, look at Joe X, he is always drunk." Or, "Look at the other guy at the end of the bar, now there's an alcoholic." A "not me," them attitude. This person is in stage two, projection of the syndrome.

Time passes and the alcoholic identifies with the status of being drunk and might say, "O.K., so I'm an alcoholic. I can handle it. Leave me alone." This is stage three, identification with the syndrome.

Eventually some individuals may find themselves going to a twelve-step meeting, and clearly and loudly stating, "I am an alcoholic." Here we have the alcoholic in stage four, confronting the syndrome.

Individuals who can take on the work in this fourth stage, confrontation, can grow into the transformation or transcendency of the syndrome. The process of confrontation with the in-depth meaning of the symbol helps the individual understand and carry their syndrome, giving them insight to meaning and purpose.

We know that not all individuals who suffer from alcoholism can move into the confrontation stage. Some try for years and cannot reach this successfully, while some remain in stage one for their lifetime. It could occur that another alcoholic thrives in stage two, the projection stage, or one might find an alcoholic confined in stage three, identification. Psychologies are different, and vary in what they can handle and achieve, regardless of what therapists and loved ones desire of them. However, to reach the stage of the individual carrying the syndrome and not having the syndrome carry the individual, one must be capable of thinking and working symbolically with confrontation of the syndrome. In the case of the apotemnophile, this would mean that the individual needs to work symbolically with the amputation desire, seeking meaning and purpose, incorporating this content and living it outwardly in the world.

To do this, the following could occur. We need to bring Jung's four stages into the understanding of the syndrome that the apotemnophile is encountering. Accompanying these stages, comprehension and differentiation between a sign and symbol must exist.

An amputee wannabe frequently reports that when they first realized this desire within themselves, they were younger and at one time or another they denied its existence. This is stage one, denial of the syndrome. They hoped for it to go away, and often tried to sublimate its hold onto them. This denial stage varies in time length among individual psychologies.

Stage two is when the apotemnophile begins to project the desired want onto another, projection of the syndrome. In stage two, they see an amputee that they feel is a representative of what they desire to become, and may follow the individual, fantasize the individual in their minds, and could even collect pictures of amputees.

During this projection phase some apotemnophiles cease projecting and they begin to identify with the amputee that they had been projecting onto. This is stage three, identification of the syndrome. (It is interesting to consider, that if the individual suffering from this syndrome does not move to stage three of identification, they remain in stage two, projection of the syndrome, and become what is known as a devotee. See Chapter 4, Question # 3.)

On the other hand, movement into stage three, identification, allows for entry into the apotemnophile's psyche that they *are* the other, the other is to be their identity, and soon the individual becomes owned by the visual representation, as sign, of the amputee. This identification, stage three, devours them and they feel a relief only if the accomplishment of the amputation would occur. They see this as the only remission, and therefore seek amputation to complete their identification with the sign, that possesses them. It is within this stage that the apotemnophile can actually hurt themselves, they are psychically overpowered by the identification with the amputee and endanger their lives by using a shotgun to destroy their healthy limb, or they have even been known to throw themselves under a passing train. The identification with the inner picture of the amputee, stage three, will be satisfying if achieved. The person caught in this stage cannot move into stage four of confrontation of the syndrome.

Stage four requires symbolic thinking. If the individual psyche does not want to think symbolically, or the individual psyche is undeveloped and unequipped to think and work symbolically, the individual will remain in stage three, identifying with the desired visual representation, as a sign, of the amputee and wanting to become it. Jungian psychology informs us that not all individual psychologies can analyze and work at this in-depth symbolic level. Thus, there are people who will be in stage three of identification and the only recourse for them is surgery, where they will find meaning and purpose for their life path. It could be that when they have acquired this satisfaction, they can move beyond this stage into the final stage of symbolic work of confrontation which includes, transcendency and transformation.

Some apotemnophiles remain caught in stage three, and cannot move from seeing the sign, to its meaning as a symbol, thus holding them back from psychological in-depth growth. Over the years of my work in this field, I have met a few individuals who have succeeded in gaining an amputation, which I analyzed as their being caught in stage three, identification. At that time they could not move into symbolic thinking and were caught in the sign as the amputee. Seeing these individuals age, I witnessed their entry into a deeper level of meaning, purpose and understanding, and they did, with time, move into stage four of symbolic work and could confront the syndrome. This has been wonderful to observe; yet these individuals never once regretted their amputation request, desire, or accomplishment, which led them into this growth process. They considered their amputation a "minor inconvenience" to the suffering and possession which they experienced earlier in life.

The wannabe desires the amputee image. On the other hand, the trauma-inflicted amputee has made the image real and may be unconcerned with its symbolic meaning. Those who have achieved amputation, either surgically or self-inflicted, state that the meaning, consequences and the inconvenience of the amputation are insignificant to them, compared to the drive which led them to become an amputee.

Now let us explore how the amputee wannabe wants the limb removed, essentially, because it was removed from them symbolically, earlier in life, and why they have a deep inner need to return to the original status.

The reader should be aware of a few factors to be able to comprehend this process. <u>First</u>, one must accept that the psyche is a VALID and REAL component in a human being's life. We are not just consciousness, or just body, but psyche at an unconscious level is present, too. <u>Second,</u> one must accept that the unconscious deals with symbols that contain real content. This unconscious content can be found in dreams, slips of the tongue, accidents, etc. <u>Third</u>, the psyche and body are in communication with each other continuously. Thus, one's psychology, or psyche, and body, or soma, are seen and described as psychosomatic. The inner connection of psyche and soma, mind and body does exist.

Now, let us see how this applies to the apotemnophiliac who searches and is driven to obtain the amputee body form. This understanding will also provide insight into the pretender and devotee's psychological need of development.

The apotemnophiliac desires to be limbless, in one way or another. He or she is responding to realize the desire held in the unconscious. How can this be if the individual presently has all healthy limbs? Remembering that the psyche is made up of unconscious content which continuously plays on consciousness, the individual may have had the experience of being loved, wanted, desired, or cherished when he or she was sacrificed or being diminished as a child. In other words, the child, when growing up, could have been squelched, belittled, denied, even violated, while being loved and accepted during this encounter or immediately after it. The child would be hurt, but the distress or injury would be balanced with preference, concern, attraction, and endearment. Confusing to the child? Yes. Disabling to the child? Very much so. The unconscious acts in symbols, and thus it could cause one to be disabled in some way.

Most apotemnophiliacs report their first sighting of an amputee occurring at age 4, 5, or 6. They recall the experience. What could be happening is that the visual representation of the amputee stays in the psyche correlating with the child's experience of being dismembered in the injurious experience of family or environment. This theory answers several other questions and explains why so often apotemnophiliacs are so kind, giving, and go out of their way to help and do for others, at their own psychic expense. They have not discovered how to achieve their own desire to live and become what it is that they want in life. It is not that they cannot become contributing individuals in this world. Often they have, but at an expense of giving something up in themselves. They sacrifice, even dismember themselves psychologically to help and do for others. Often they don't know how to say "no" to others, because to do so would be treating others as they were first treated themselves. They do not want to become what was hurtful to themselves. This also applies to wannabes, devotees, and pretenders (see Chapter IV, Questions # 2, # 3, # 4). However, this could be experienced in the reverse, which Jung would call a compensatory response. The apotemnophiliac would present himself or herself as argumentative, feisty, opinionated, stubborn, or difficult.

Before closing this section on Jung's insights, Aniela Jaffe, a Jungian analyst who wrote *Memories, Dreams and Reflections* with Dr. Jung gave insight into Jung's theory of Individuation and the mandala. Aniela reported on a mandala that Jung had seen and spoken to her about. It was not quite the norm for a mandala in that the colors and shapes were not uniformly opposite to each other, in perfect symmetry, as most mandalas are. Jung told Aniela Jaffe that some psyches existed like this mandala and that this was a balance for them. In other words, an individual psyche could appear off-balanced to someone else, yet for that particular psyche it is a balanced and harmonious state, similar to the mandala she was showing. Apotemmnophiles may be a walking copy of that mandala. (Note: book cover.)

Self-mutilating Behavior

Harper (1996) reports that trauma theory psychologists (Briere, Herman, Miller, Shengold) find a high correlation between self-destructive behaviors and severe abuse, neglect in childhood, and failure to have formed secure attachments. Many view these behaviors as an attempt to fill a void, escape emptiness, express emotional pain, and ease tension. This could explain why some women who suffer from self-mutilating behavior find healing when having their first baby, and why some individuals who marry and have relatedness find structure that helps them resolve their self-mutilating behavior.

According to Herman (1992), self-mutilating behavior is not done to "manipulate" others (p. 109). Some people may request amputation as a way to make themselves dependent which is a form of manipulation of relatives or caregivers. We know from experience that those who dismember and those who are apotemnophiliacs most frequently do this in private and keep it secretive. Miller (1994) finds destructive urges to be adaptive and basic to "survival skills" (p. 9). Childhood conditions and self-mutilation could have some correlation. For example, loss of a parent is one of the most profound traumas a child can experience. Any parental loss and separation could result in psychological symptoms later in life. Walsh and Rosen (1988) indicate that several authors (Kafka, Pao, Asch, Friedman) believe that parental loss and/or loss of a significant other could set up the dynamics for self-mutilating acts to begin. Additionally, Walsh and Rosen (1988) "note that several empirical studies (Rosenthal, *et al*, 1972; Simpson, 1975; Carol, *et al*, and Sweeny and Zamecnik, 1981) of adult mutilators have linked loss with self-mutilator behaviors" (p. 60). However, parental loss alone seems "unlikely to produce self-mutilation" (p. 61), and they report that Friedman *et al* proposed that hatred of one's body "in an intense self-alienated way" (p. 61) could be the key stimulus to this behavior. Most apotemnophiliacs view their body in a distorted way, disoriented from the way they actually present themselves. They do not like what they have as a body and want to be missing a limb. This theory of the loss of parenting and dislike of body go hand in hand. Apotemnophiliacs do not want to parent themselves in the body form they have, and demand surgery to create a new body form. The renewal of an acceptable body form, such as an amputee, would allow the apotemnophiliacs to now parent themselves and care for themselves in an appropriate manner. In reality, this is what occurs. Once amputation has occurred, apotemnophiliacs take good care of themselves and venture into life with full force, not as disabled second-class citizens, but rather as able-bodied, self-fulfilled individuals, supporting themselves and family via work and parenting.

Another insight is that mutilators could have learned to self-mutilate via observation of parents' behavior; however, according to research from Walsh and Rosen (1988) parental role modeling is "not sufficient to account for self-mutilating behavior in offspring" (pp. 61-64). The above developmental findings lend credence to Peters' (1994) very convincing assertion that, "These self-destructive symptoms are thus actually attempts at self-transformation or 'rites of passage,' as Reeves and Tugend (1988) say, that have 'gone wrong'" (p. 6). Viewing one's body in a self-alienated way prepares the self-mutilator to take action in a self-transformative way. Apotemnophiliacs do not regard their activities as self-mutilating, but rather as correction of a "mutilation" – the conversion to what they regard as their correct body image.

Favazza (1996) states,

> Self-mutilation cannot be understood without recourse to psychology, biology and culture. ...self-mutilation not only is a pathological behavior but also an expression of a struggle to re-enter a "normal" life. ...self-mutilators seek what we all seek: an ordered life, spiritual peace—maybe even salvation—and a healthy mind in a healthy body. These desperate methods are upsetting to those of us who try to achieve these goals in a more tranquil manner, but the methods rest firmly on the dimly perceived bedrock of the human experience. (pp. 322-323)

Our body is the link between ourselves (our inner world), our souls, and the outer world. We use our body to project ourselves into the outer social world, and we use our body to bring the unconscious content into consciousness. The ideas of how we should look are developed by the outer world.

Lincoln (1981) writes in <u>Emerging from the Chrysalis: Studies in Rituals of Women's Initiation:</u>

> In a very concrete sense, responsibility for the fertility of people and crops thus evolves upon Tiv women when they receive their scars. …One might even go so far as to argue that scarification makes every woman into an Akomobo (sacred object), makes every woman into the Imborivungu (owl pipe), makes every woman into the tar (the land). Four lines cut at puberty make a woman the guardian of fertility and well-being, heir of the past and creator of the future. The scars themselves are simultaneously the means of her transformation and the visible mark that this transformation has been completed, making each girl a woman and a sacred object for all to see. (p. 49)

Could this not be what apotemnophiliacs search for? The amputation they experience within their psyche and on their body is their mark that "transformation has been completed," marking them as man or woman and more importantly, feeling as if they are "a sacred object." This would account for the very high rate of satisfaction that wannabes experience after gaining their desired amputations. The psyche, for whatever reason, be it from the collective psychoid realm or from the personal realm, finally gains fulfillment.

Victoria Ebin (1979) in <u>The Body Decorated</u>, cites J.C. Beaglehole's report of Captain Cook's 1769 journey in <u>The Voyage of the Endeavour</u>, noting that "both sexes paint their bodies *Tattow*, as it is called in their language. This is done by inlaying the Colour of black under their skins in such a manner as to be indelible" (p. 5). This voyage allowed one culture of consciousness to enter into another culture of consciousness, and then the question, of whether it was acceptable or not, arose. Ebin also shows how efforts were made to indoctrinate one's own values of the collective and to "prohibit the 'natives' from carrying out ritual practices, such as body decoration, [as] a necessary step in demolishing the structure of their traditional belief" (p. 6). It is interesting to note that while explorers and missionaries were encountering tribal peoples, curiosity surrounding adornments, surgical operations, circumcision rites, and scarring techniques were recorded simultaneously as these foreign intruders attempted to extinguish these practices. Returning to Jung's theory of the collective unconscious, could it be that self-mutilators are connected to these earlier generations psychologically via the collective unconscious and are re-enacting their ritualistic stand? Content from the collective unconscious is overflowing and cannot be contained by the ego.

Edinger (1972) in Ego and Archetype, states that a normal

> reaction to an excessive and irrational rejection is characteristic, namely, violence. Whenever one experiences an unbearable alienation and despair it is followed by violence. The violence can take either an external or an internal form. In extreme forms this means either murder or suicide. The crucial point is that at the root of the violence of any form lies the experience of alienation—a rejection too severe to be endured. (p. 44)

This helps us understand that relatedness can heal self-mutilators' behavior. If self-mutilators have relatedness, alienation and rejection are not so severe, thus allowing individuals to accept themselves inwardly. The questions to consider here are: is this ever too late, and does the wannabe want this? Regardless of age, apotemnophiliacs state that they cannot find steadiness within, at this point, to find a satisfying relationship. Once they achieve their surgery, they feel they will be better able to be involved in relationships. This is proven in cases where surgery has been successful.

Edinger (1972) continues and says,

> alienation is an archetypal and hence a generally human experience, exaggerated forms of the experience... are usually found in people with a certain type of traumatic childhood. In cases where the child experiences a severe degree of rejection by the parents, the ego-Self axis is damaged and the child is then predisposed in later life to states of alienation which can reach unbearable proportions. This course of events is due to the fact that the child experiences parental rejection as rejection by God. The experience is then built into the psyche as permanent ego-Self alienation.
>
> In the context of Christian psychology, the alienation experience is commonly understood as divine punishment for sin. (pp. 54-55)

This gives credibility to the earlier information on loss of parenting as a traumatic childhood condition. Thus, mutilating behavior could be occurring in clients as a talisman, representing and substituting for their inner work. The symbolism is that self-mutilation carries energy substituting for the lack of inner processing of attempts to relate to the outer world, past and present. This certainly supports the secretive nature of self-mutilating behavior and that of the apotemnophiliac. For the self-mutilator, who is open about the desire, the mutilating behavior has a chance to subside. The more open and the more at ease the self-mutilator is with befriending this behavior, the less the behavior owns the individual and the less it has to be acted out. Peters (1994), citing Frank, says, "rituals heal because their purpose is to create social support and thereby decrease alienation, encouraging hope and faith which, in turn, reduces depression and anxiety" (p. 7). Perhaps the client should not substitute the ritual of self-mutilation for relatedness. Perhaps apotemnophiliacs are in the "same set of shoes." If these individuals could find inner and outer relatedness, then transformation can occur, and the self-mutilating behavior, the desire for amputation, can subside. A new ritual of relatedness must grow—the ingredients for this, as suggested by Estes (1992) are *suffering, striving, and endurance.* Jung (1969) concurs with this theory because he claims that "neurosis is always a substitute for legitimate suffering" (p. 28).

Ross and McKay (1979) state: "Self-mutilation is found widely in the literature of anthropology, suicidology, criminology, psychiatry, psychology, dermatology, sociology, epidemiology, theology, psychoanalysis, and plastic surgery" (p. 19). This has been a dramatic behavior deep in the human psyche for ages, and seems to be universal (archetypal). Therefore, many people know a mutilator or they themselves have mutilator qualities.

It could be possible that each of us is born with the history of our elders within us at the collective unconscious level (Jung, 1966). In development of the Self, perhaps special content from the collective unconscious escapes into consciousness. If the ego is not acting appropriately as an ordering, organizing center, this escaped content could overwhelm the ego and act in possession of the individual, thus, living out the unconscious content in an individual's life. Or, it is a calling of the self to incorporate it into one's life, and a ritual passage is required.

Erich Neuman (1954) a student of Jung, suggests in The Origins and History of Consciousness that ritual, as

> evidenced of initiation rites whose purpose it was...to transform the initiate into the higher man and so make him akin to, or identical with, God. ...whether the celebrant is seized with ecstasy and becomes *'entheos,'* or is ritually regenerated, or takes God into his own body through communion with him, always the goal is the higher man, the attainment of his spiritual, heavenly part. As the Gnostics of a later day expressed it, the initiate becomes an *'ennoos,'*

> one who possesses nous, or who, the nous possesses, a *'pneumatiko.'* (Concerning Rebirth, p.253)

The amputation need is a "rite of renewal," concerning "rebirth," and thus far the handful of individuals who have acquired the desired surgery all report feeling "reborn." They demonstrate a zest to begin life anew. Their only regret is that they did not do this earlier. This ritual of "rebirth" allows the apotemnophiliac to establish a new perspective, following most psychological theories that agree that what is inside individuals is projected outward into their lives.

Jung (1969) writes, in <u>Psychology and Religion,</u>

> In general, flaying signifies transformation from a worse state to a better, and hence renewal and rebirth. The best examples are to be found in the religion of ancient Mexico. Thus, in order to renew the moon-goddess a young woman was decapitated and skinned, and a youth then put the skin round him to represent the risen goddess. The prototype of this renewal is the snake casting its skin every year, a phenomenon round which primitive fantasy has always played. (p. 228)

An elective amputation takes the client from a perceived worse state to a better state. It reflects a new inner perspective, and regardless of what others want to tell the apotemnophiliac to believe, the client finds renewal, joy, contentment, wholeness, and happiness in the new body alignment.

If this ritual has meaning and works positively for apotemnophiliacs, we may need to help these individuals follow their desire. Jung (1953) states in <u>Psychology and Alchemy,</u> "Had these rites of renewal not yielded definite results they would not only have died out in prehistoric times but would never have arisen in the first place" (p. 137).

Apotemnophiliacs experience "deprivation of maternal love and parental rejection in early childhood" (Bruno, 1997, p. 251). This does not just mean the parent was absent, but can be so subtle that the child ends up parenting the parent, and enantiodromia occurs where the situation goes to the opposite extreme. The child takes this job on out of fear of being abandoned, lost, or left by death. The child may parent the mother if the father leaves the family. The timing and responsibility of the child's psyche, connected with the mother's need and the father's exit, is what triggers the alienation of the child's Self-axis and mutilating, annihilating actions seem to substitute for want, love, parenting, care, and wholeness.

Relatedness

Let us return to the problem of relatedness. The mutilators, and apotemnophiliacs are not in an appropriate child-parent relationship and respond in an annihilating way to themselves. Another child in the same situation may move towards alcoholism or whatever, as the symbol for what the loss represents. Why? Could it be that the symbol corresponds most appropriately to the circumstances of the child's life and governs the timing and placement of the cathecting of the psychic energy. So many apotemnophiliacs report that their first desire, or a sighting of an amputee, was around age four or five. According to Freud, developmentally, this is the age of the Electra Complex/Oedipus Complex that coincides with the Castration complex. So while the child is falling in love with the opposite sex parent, the child is threatened by the same sex parent, and the psyche cannot handle this annihilation. Waiting for the loss could be too great. The child does not wait. Instead, the child enacts it via mutilation or amputation. The pressure, the obsession at a psychic level is no longer there, because the enactment has occurred. To live with the enactment is less damaging than the threat that is always "hanging in the air." This could be why apotemnophiliacs report that living with the amputation is easier than living with the obsessive-compulsive drive demanding it.

Jung suggests that we look at fairy tales and myths, which contain content from the unconscious, to understand the process of one's psyche. Fairy tales are often universal and have much to teach about the collective. Estes (1994) suggests that the motif of cutting as initiation is central to the development of the feminine. In the fairy tale, *The Handless Maiden*, the symbol of the tree is related to the great wild mother and is symbolic of the "concept of the young sapling pruned with an ax in order to grow more full" (p. 406). Real trees, when pruned, can die and return to life. The tale dealing with the dismembering of the maiden's hands, illustrates taking away her ability to hold, grasp, control, and do things, and psychically, she loses the ability "to grasp, to hold and to help herself" (p. 405) in the manner she has learned. This ability dies, and she must journey and find her own way of grasping life anew. Estes (1992) suggests that an act of cutting, scarification, tattooing, dismembering, or any act to self-disintegrate is an act of its opposite—to return to growing and developing. Apotemnophiliacs who have their amputations feel success and happiness. They do not see themselves as disabled, but as able-bodied, their return to growing and developing. The amputation is the beginning of an initiation, the process by which we turn from our natural inclination to remain unconscious, into consciousness. To travel this journey into *suffering, striving, and endurance,* we find conscious union with the deeper Self. This fairy tale analysis is yet another example supporting a rite of passage in the individual's development. Eliade (1964) points out in his writing on shamanism that the central theme to initiation is "dismemberment of the neophyte's body and renewal of (their) organs; ritual death followed by resurrection" (p. 38).

Elder (1996) writes in <u>An Encyclopedia of Archetypal Symbolism: The Body</u>, of an interesting finding which correlates with Estes (1994). While referring to body painting, or to more permanent forms of body decorating, such as tattooing and scarification, he says,

> Whatever the technique (with the exception of modern electrical equipment), it is always an

> extremely painful ordeal to be tattooed, a fact that points to the great importance of this practice in rites of initiation. Tattooing proves to be a test of one's *endurance* and a permanent record, should one be successful, that one has *endured;* the pain is symbolic of the 'death' of an old status making way for the 'new being'—the adult, the warrior, the married woman. And that new status is as indelible as the tattoos [scarring, amputation, etc., whatever change of body form] themselves. (pp.60-61)

Virel (1980), in <u>Ritual and Seduction: The Human Body As Art</u>, teaches that rituals are the handwriting of myths, which are the analogies of human life. He further says that religion and magic have ritual in common, and ritual provides a way for all to share in the divine. Body adornment is the communion and ritual is the vehicle. This seems to illustrate that perhaps clients psychically caught in self-mutilation patterns might be attempting to reach the divine via a ritual acting out. They may be caught in one of the stages of the ritual and cannot transcend to the next stage, thus repeating the self-mutilating pattern. Joseph Campbell (1973) suggests that there were three stages in a ritual: separation, initiation, and return. Mutilators and apotemnophiliacs may be caught in the initiation phase, repeating it over and over, incapable of reaching or entering the return phase. To do so would mean they would have to let the initiate in them die, entering responsibly as new individuals in the outer world, carrying a new status.

Eliade (1987), in <u>The Encylopedia of Religion,</u> writes that the body is constantly being altered naturally and culturally. Biological growth leaves marks on the body, adolescence brings about changes, aging develops the body in another fashion, and furthermore, "accidents at work and play mar, scar, mutilate and deform the body" (p. 269). These happenings could be brought about via "invisible beings or powers, such as deities, ancestors, or witchcraft" (p. 269). Thus, supernormal powers can be attributed to the lame, to the deformed, or marred individuals.

Individuals who are caught in the psychic possession of self-mutilating behavior may be acting in a religious fashion, being called by these deities, ancestors, or witches, and may need extraordinary ego strength to pay tribute to these callings without necessarily being swallowed up by them.

This research seems to indicate that perhaps the loss of one's Self, or, loss of the relatedness to one's Self, may be important reasons to consider in a client's mutilating or apotemnophiliac behavior. Furthermore, body piercing and tattooing are extremely prevalent among young people today. This could be because relatedness to the Self is lacking for two reasons: 1) it is more difficult to find because of the lack of close "parenting," and, 2) in today's world a developed concept of Self is demanded of the individual at an increasingly younger age.

CHAPTER III
CASE STUDIES

Case 1

The client, a 63-year-old male, was hospitalized for a self-inflicted chain-saw wound to his leg. A witness to the incident called the emergency squad. The client, when later confronted with the eyewitness report, admitted to self-inflicting the wound. He described a deep-seated, unexplainable feeling that had lived inside him for years, that he could no longer control it, and had to take action. He planned the incident precisely, close to his home, with a tourniquet readily available to stop profuse bleeding. He planned to call the hospital for assistance, but his cell phone was not accessible. He reported that he had considered medication for pain management, but decided against it, in case hospital staff might get overly suspicious.

Upon assessment, the client admitted having this unexplainable inner compulsion to have his leg amputated since childhood. He had dealt with the guilt of this urge years earlier. This was his fourth attempt to damage his leg. Previous attempts were fruitless and less significant. Doctors healed the infection or wound before amputation was necessary. During one hospitalization he pleaded with the doctors to amputate because of pain, but he was referred to a psychiatrist and given drugs for his discomfort.

He was determined that his fourth attempt would sufficiently damage the vascular vessels, making amputation unavoidable. He succeeded and, of course, after surgery, he was sent for a psychiatric evaluation and consult. He did not see this action as a choice. He felt driven within. He knew he could no longer live carrying the compulsion and that this was either going to succeed or he would eventually take his own life to end the suffering. In short, this was an act of desperation, not to die, but to live as he felt he was meant to live. The diagnosis was that he suffered from Body dysmorphic disorder. He was released from the hospital and no charges were brought against him.

When interviewed, this client appeared calm, very cooperative, well informed and considerate. He wanted to help others with the same diagnosis to avoid the same unbearable pain. He had a graduate degree and was retired, but worked part time to keep busy. He was seeing a therapist, as he had done on and off for years, working on relationship issues with his children and ex-wife. He also had concerns with siblings over inheritance and property, but overall seemed very well adjusted to his physical situation concerning the amputation. He reported that "well adjusted" was not the norm for him before the amputation. He described himself, in previous years, as nervous, agitated, and difficult for others to live with, as well as difficult to live with himself. For the years he had sought surgery for the wanted amputation, he felt frustrated, unheard, and demeaned. Doctors refused assistance and advised him to seek psychiatric help.

The client described his amputation as a "minor inconvenience," compared to the major "compelling drive" for amputation with which he had lived for so many years. He admitted to enjoying life as an amputee, taking his time doing whatever he wanted, and finally "feeling total, whole." His only regret was that he had not succeeded in obtaining an amputation earlier in life and that he had to wait until in his sixties to achieve such satisfaction.

He did not care if others talked about him or knew the truth concerning his amputation. He wore shorts and showed his prosthesis openly, and did not care that people might think him odd or peculiar because of this. He delighted in talking to children about his wooden leg, and found that most adults had more problems with his amputation than did the children. He understood how others could not comprehend what he had done, but his need for surgical removal of his leg was a mystery to him too. Since childhood, the feeling was "a very alive urge" which he felt compelled to act on. The big issue for him was a moral one. He felt it was a taboo in his culture to do harm to his body (which he disliked doing), but the medical world had refused to help him obtain an amputation and he found no other avenue open to him. At that point, he submitted to the possessive drive and enacted his successful plan, which led to the desired consequence. Nevertheless, he violated a taboo and has had to deal with the burden of this. Freud (1964) pointed out, to include the aggressive, destructive nature into the "human constitution appears sacrilegious; it contradicts too many religious presumptions and social conventions" (p. 104), which is exactly what this individual suffered.

Today he is happy, willing to communicate with other apotemnophiliacs, and supportive of them in their efforts to achieve amputation. He will advise them on cautions to consider, but will not personally take any action to help them harm themselves. He stresses the need for continuing to work with the medical community to enlighten it about this affliction, with the hope that doctors and staff will make themselves available for requested surgeries. His great wish is that eventually, someday, the insight of what this philia is about will be "out in the open" and the terror of its burden can be lifted from many individuals.

Case 2

The client was a 57-year-old male, well educated, who claimed to be a "wannabe" amputee since age 7. He had reported his life desire to his therapist and sought many avenues for legitimate amputation of his leg. He sought medical help from his physician and from physicians at private clinics. They all advised counseling. In one situation, the surgeon with whom he spoke chased him from the clinic after he made his request for surgery. He reported that another clinic agreed to his requested surgery, but, after they took his money, they avoided him and said they did not know what he was talking about. He had no grounds to press charges and had to leave this situation unresolved. The burden of carrying this compulsion overwhelmed him, and finally prompted him to use an electric jigsaw to sever his ankle. He was hospitalized for several weeks, which included a psychiatric evaluation and assessment. He stuck to his story that this was an accident and nothing was ever done about the incident.

The frustration continued and he contacted a surgeon who worked in a third world country. After a few consultations, the surgeon agreed to the surgery. The client paid for the surgery, and the procedure was done shortly after agreement. The amputation was successful, but the client died a week later due to complications that the surgeon could not curtail. It was a third world clinic with limited facilities and medicines. Necessary medications were not available to prevent further complications and the patient, subsequently, died. One conjectures that if this surgery had been completed in a reputable hospital with appropriate facilities and medicines, more than likely, the client would be alive today.

This client reported before he went for his surgery that he would risk his life, because the terror and horror which he was feeling when he woke up every morning in the wrong body form was more agonizing than death. He felt it was his last hope.

There are other reported cases of apotemnophiliacs who have died attempting to reach their goal of living in a body that is not foreign to them. They state that they are seeking a calm, healthy mental and physical acceptance of themselves, and believe it can only be achieved through amputation of an undesired limb.

Case 3

The client was a 47-year-old male, married with two children, a blue-collar worker in a middle class community. The man actively sought help several times from orthopedic surgeons who, in all cases, refused to amputate. Several surgeons recommended counseling and referred him to a psychiatrist. One surgeon eventually said that if a competent psychiatrist affirmed the need for amputation, then something might become available. The client sought counseling and did receive a letter of recommendation for amputation of a healthy limb. After an extensive evaluation with medical boards and further psychiatric evaluations and assessments, the surgery was arranged, delayed, re-arranged and delayed, because of hospital schedules and doctors wanting to further debate the procedure. The medical community, after verifying that the client had attempted other avenues for resolution, performed the surgery, and the patient had his leg amputated as requested.

Hospital confinement was brief (research shows that a client's attitude toward amputation has a positive effect on recovery time). Within weeks the client was in rehabilitation and within two months was walking about on a prosthesis. He returned to work, having adjusted to compensate for his amputation. His immediate family knew of this elective amputation and accepted it as part of who he was. They have seen a remarkable change in him for the good. His friends, fellow employees and employer now have information of the apotemnophilia desire and have accepted that his leg difficulties required amputation. They report he is working well and is as efficient as he was before the surgery. Both family and workers communicate that the client has a different attitude, and is more related in his approach to others and to himself. Some individuals, who do not know of the apotemnophilia request, wonder if the shock of amputation is what changed his attitude and disposition. The family and client report greater happiness, an excitement toward life, and greater calmness in living than before the surgery.

The findings in this case are consistent with other apotemnophiliacs who have undergone self-inflicted traumatic experiences ending in amputation of a limb or digit. After the amputation they can get on with life, free of the burden of the alien extension of their body, and they can and do, finally, live freely and happily.

Case 4

This 35-year-old male desired an above knee amputation. This wannabe desperation drove him to search for competent doctors, who refused assistance. When he could not tolerate the possession any longer, he learned from a doctor what to inject to deaden his leg nerves. He injected himself. A companion, who originally rejected his plea for help, agreed, eventually, to help, because it was so obvious how much the client was suffering. The leg was hacked off below the knee, bludgeoned, and tossed away. The instruments were hidden in the desert. The client was rushed to a hospital, where he claimed that he had been in a motor bike accident. Hospital personnel could only clean the wound and help him heal. Later, he went back for revision surgery to become an above-knee amputee, which is what he desired, but many surgeons would not help him with this request. Finally, a surgeon asked for a psychiatric evaluation and, with the psychiatric recommendation, performed the requested revision. This male has been living life very happily ever since.

Case 5

In November 1999, two messages on the Internet in which assistance was sought for doing harm in hopes of acquiring amputation.

The first message was from a wannabe:

"Does anyone know if a 'staph' infection would lead to amputation?"

The second message was a request:

"Could you suggest ideas on what to do and how I could achieve being a DBE (double below-elbow amputee) without also endangering my life?"

Case 6

A 33-year-old man reported how he was taken advantage because he acted foolishly, out of despair. He had, finally, met another male wannabe seeking amputation and he formed a friendship in which he thought there was a trust. He decided to attempt to damage his leg. His acquaintance agreed to assist. But, after money was exchanged to arrange for the equipment, the acquaintance disappeared. The man reported that he was willing to trust anyone who would help him achieve his desire. A few years have passed and both men still desire surgery, but the trust between them has been destroyed.

These case studies illustrate the extreme extent of desperate action that apotemnophiliacs will take to achieve their desire and fulfill their inner calling. It is not something easily put aside. It is demanded from within the soul. The psychological suffering is so great that some clients induce this horrible self injury in hopes of obtaining their desired end result of amputation. These cases request that the medical community reconsider declining such requests for amputation that have psychiatric validation and recommendation. Surgeons and hospital administrators must begin to recognize and respect their psychiatric colleagues who approve and advocate amputation for selected patients. Otherwise, more and more despair and anxiety will result in apotemnophiliacs performing reckless and imprudent physically destructive acts upon their being. Hope lies in the education of the medical profession a growing consciousness regarding apotemnophilia.

CHAPTER IV
QUESTIONS AND ANSWERS

1. What is apotemnophilia?

Apotemnophilia describes a syndrome in which individuals believe they belong in a body that is missing a limb or a digit, or, in other words, a body different from their four normal limbs. Because most are caught in a body form that does not comply with this design, they elect to lose a limb or have a body part surgically removed. Those diagnosed with this compulsive condition often damage or maim themselves in order to require amputation by a surgeon. They see and feel themselves living life more acceptably as an amputee. The term was first applied to this compulsion in a 1977 article entitled, "Apotemnophilia: Two Cases of Self-Demand Amputation as a Paraphilia," by J. Money, R. Jobaris, and G. Furth.

This compulsion is the identity for which the individual strives. Living life as an amputee is an identity which apotemnophiliacs feel is their natural body form and their natural way. Apotemnophilia is not about becoming disabled; it is, instead, about becoming able-bodied and feeling whole in relation to the person within. As noted earlier, apotemnophiles are not about sexual gratification, but about the arousal of their identity as a fully functioning human being that they know they can be.

Apotemnophiliacs differ in what they are seeking and in ranges of desire. Some apotemnophiliacs want only a digit or a portion of a finger or toe removed. Once this is accomplished, it satisfies them, and they accept their new body form. Others feel they need the loss of an entire limb, often a leg. They feel this need to gain acceptance of themselves living in their body form. Other apotemnophiliacs desire bilateral amputation of upper or lower limbs, or a combination of one and the other. Apotemnophiles often work towards having an entire limb amputated, either by self inflicting damage to the limb which results in amputation, or by seeking medical help which, thus far, has not been available. Thus, they put themselves in life threatening situations. The term used to describe those desiring surgical removal of a digit or limb is "wannabe."

2. What is a wannabe?

A wannabe is usually a non-disabled individual who wants to become an individual with a physical disability. Wannabes see themselves in a body that is not fully functioning, and they strive to become the image that they believe they are. This is, most frequently, as an amputee or a paraplegic. Sexual fetishism is unrelated to this status of being. An apotemnophile wannabe is not sexually oriented, they are about finding identity.

3. What is a devotee?

A devotee, is usually, a non-disabled individual who has a special interest in, and/or is sexually attracted to people who are disabled. Attraction to disabilities can range from a major amputation of limb (leg amputation seems to be most common), to finger, arm, or toe loss, broken limbs set in plaster casts, any physical deformities, hearing loss, paraplegia (partial or full), orthodonture loss, blindness, or individuals confined to a wheelchair. Most frequently, the majority of devotees are men interested in women. However, there are women who are attracted to disabled men, and this syndrome exists in the heterosexual, homosexual, and bisexual worlds. A devotee could also be a wannabe.

4. What is a pretender?

A pretender is, usually, a non-disabled individual who lives as if they have a disability. Pretenders use paraphernalia to make the experience realistic. For example, an individual who believes he/she should be a paraplegic will have a wheelchair, crutches, or leg braces, and will go out in public with these appliances or use them in private in daily living. Pretender paraplegics can confine themselves to their chairs full time and never walk. These individuals report that they are very happy with their life in the chair as compared to when they were not confined to it. They often use excuses, such as leg problems caused by diabetes. The pretender amputee has a more difficult time trying to be an amputee and feels frustrated and dissatisfied. This often leads to a physical act of injury and personal violence. There are reported cases where the pretender/wannabe amputee inflicted self-injury and died in an attempt to become an amputee.

5. What are wannabes on the internet sharing?

During the period from 1994 to 1999, the following comments were solicited as part of subscribing to an Internet e-mail list (http://www.angelfire.com/or/want2be/) devoted to discussing the desire to become an amputee. All references that might reveal an individual's identity have been removed. The comments provide a representative cross-section view of wannabe individuals in their own words. It is particularly interesting that these comments read more like those of a transgendered person rather than those of a person intent on mutilation. For example, a transgendered person might describe himself/herself this way:

> All my life I've known that I was a woman. I tried to talk to my friends about it and they would make fun of me. The other boys were out playing war games and all I wanted to do was cook and play with dolls. Now that I've had my surgery, I feel complete.

A psychotic person might say:
My hand was always offending me. It would make me shop lift. I knew what I had to do, I had read it in the bible. I cut my hand off

and threw it in the lake. I could not believe that
I continued to shop lift.

An apotemnophiliac might say:
All my life I've known that I was supposed
to have one leg. I was too terrified to tell
anyone. I did tell a very close friend and they
never talked to me again. I loved to stand in
front of a mirror with my leg folded up so I
looked like I only had one leg. When I saw an
amputee on the street, I was so jealous, but I
knew that someday I would be like that. I would
pretend as often as I could, but it was not the
same. Now that I really have only one leg, I feel
complete.

Comments from apotemnophiliac wannabe people over the Internet:

This is something that I've thought about for
many years. Realistically, I don't know if I
would ever act, and probably couldn't get the
deed done, even if I wanted to. Nonetheless, it
has always been on my mind.

I've been pretending since I was very young
(kindergarten or earlier). I do it often and for
long periods of time. It sometimes becomes
disruptive, in that I will sometimes be so
compelled to pretend that I will continue to do
so at the expense of making appointments.
There have been times when I needed to go to
the grocery store because there was nothing left
to eat in the house, but I went hungry for several
days rather than quit pretending so that I could
go to the store. Pretending has also had physical
effects. My right knee (the leg I always pretend
with) is weak and often painful because of much

pretending. It is also the knee that was damaged in the auto accident, and one must wonder if it would have been as badly damaged if it were not already weakened. I know that there is a huge difference between pretending and actually being an amputee, but my pretending is and always has been such that I really regret having to stop when the need to go into public arises. The only reason I quit when I have to go out is that my place of residence is a small city, and I invariably run into people I know when I go out. These people know that I am not an amputee. If I were an amputee, there would be no problem! Another fact that might be of interest is that when I go on long road trips to places where I don't know people, I continue to pretend, even in public. It's very hard for me to explain, but somehow it seems natural; as if this were the way I was meant to be.

I'm 53, and have been a wannabe since I was a kid. It ruined a 26-year marriage.

I'm feeling a little lost and am not sure what to say. I recently discovered I'm a wannabe. I'm a nice, normal, highly functioning woman, who thought for the longest time that there was something horribly wrong with me—until I learned that there is a name for what I feel. I know I'm not "sick," and don't really feel guilty about it, but life is getting a little intolerable knowing this about myself, but not really understanding it. I don't know who else to talk to, and certainly don't want counseling. I'm hoping there will someday soon be the availability for elective surgical amputation.

As for my wish, I want to be a DAK(double above-knee). For the past 10 years or so, of the dreams I can remember, in all of them I'm in a chair. Don't know why. And all of my life I've wondered about being an amputee. . .the two sort of came together for me recently and it was like clouds opening up, letting the sun in, when I realized, that's what is right for me. I guess it's a little like someone who realizes they need a sex change. . .I never understood that before but I'm starting to see how horrible it is to feel there's something not right with your body.

I am in a quandary. I have always wanted this amputation, dreamed about it and acted it out, but now, at 56 and facing the possibility of maybe that someday this is possible, I wonder if this is what I want to do. I really know nothing about it. I know nothing about what I might be entering into. Please help me with this. You have been there. What is it like? How do you feel now that it is a fact for you that you cannot undo the bandage and "Praise the Lord," throw away your crutch and WALK. The only person I have known who was an amputee was a girl friend of a friend and I was in such awe that I was speechless around her.

I have been a LAK(left above-knee) wannabe for years. I cut my finger off last year hoping to build up enough of what it takes to cut my leg off also. Haven't done it yet. Would like to converse with others with the same inclination.

I've wanted to be a RAK(right above-knee) ever since I can remember and am just waiting for the opportunity to arise. Hopefully, this coming summer or fall, depending on my method of accidental amputation.

I'm a 26-year-old bi-male in Canada. I've always been interested in amputee guys. I particularly like finger and toe amputations, and have long wanted to have at least one of my fingers and a couple of my toes amputated. In fact, I frequently tape one or more of my fingers or toes up to resemble a stump. I occasionally pretend to be an arm amputee as well, although I doubt I would actually want to have an arm amputated.

I am not a wannabe. I know someone who has been obsessed with the desire to have both of her legs amputated for many years and she would give anything to know how this could be accomplished safely. Are there support groups available for such individuals or ways and means?

Last September I had a once-in-a-lifetime opportunity, and I took it. As a result, my right leg ends six inches above where my knee used to be. I have been spending much time recuperating and getting used to this change in life.

I have always been intensely interested in amputations. . .for as long as I can remember, and have pretended, privately to be an AK(above-knee) and AE (above-elbow). I'm sure there is some wannabe in me, but great fear of the unknown, as it were, as well. I would very much like to be able to correspond with others who feel as I do and who, perhaps, have gone farther than I. This correspondence would help me further confirm if I am a wannabe or a devotee.

I was ready to do a "major." Had it all planned out. Had everything lined up, anesthesia, equipment, even had help lined up. I had gotten in touch with you a few years before. You insisted that I talk to my significant-other, which I did. For good or for bad, she nixed the whole thing. So rather than sulk I remained determined and decided I would take what I could get and now sport this wonderful "minor" (accidents happen, you know). I'm quite satisfied. Maybe more than I dreamed possible.

I am a 27-year-old bilateral above-knee amputee wannabe/pretender/devotee. I have talked with a woman on the Internet about this desire and it helped me a lot. I need to discuss this with more people who are similar.

My girl friend is a BK(below-knee) wannabe. She needs assistance to find a suitable place to have the operation performed since she does not want to go on thinking everyday about it. After long discussion pro and con, I agreed to help her and to find a place. Could you give us any help as to where we could find a surgeon or hospital treating this syndrome.

I am very interested in the wannabe/amputee issue. There are a lot of reasons why I am interested, but the main things are that I work a lot with amputees and I recently became a DAK(double above-knee). I must admit that being an amputee is something exceptional. I don't know what it is, probably it's the same thrill that wannabes have.

I have lost much quality of life since I have the feelings of a wannabe. In the area where I live there is no means of discussing this item. I am glad I got in touch with you as it affords the opportunity for me to be open. I had the same opportunity to become an amputee but I regard this as an issue that needs to be discussed with others with the same interest. I sincerely hope you can accept me.

I am 24 years old and I live in Germany. Since I can remember I have wished to be an amputee. I am a LBK(left below-knee) wannabe.

I'm thinking I am a devotee, but somewhere in my mind I also want to be an amputee, is it the specialty to be less than the most? I'd ask myself a lot of questions and also in a depression time I tried to hurt myself, trying to become an amputee (1 or 2 arms/2 legs). It didn't happen, because it hurt too much. Since I have a new job and I see a psychologist I'm not doing these things anymore, but still there is a wish. I want to hear more about this subject. It is amazing for me to have learned that I was not the only one having devotee and wannabe feelings.

I am a DAK(double above-knee) wannabe and have been for a long time. I am 41 and wish to be a bilateral mid-thigh amputee, possibly a triple, LBE(left-below elbow). I remember being attracted to amps from as early as 12 or 13 when our neighbors uncle visited. He was a double BE(below-elbow). He let me help wash the car so I got a good look at his stumps and after, his hooks, exciting! Following that I had a friend in high school who was into devil worship, etc., and got drunk in the lotus position in an abandoned garage. He because a double below knee amputee. So he was the first my age and loved showing off his stumps in both the pool and wheelchair that he preferred to his prosthetics. I love the look of a man in a chair without legs, therefore I tend to look for AKs whenever possible and have determined after a lot of fantasy and soul searching that I could without qualm become a DAK(double above-knee). The triple aspect is more fantasy than not but I always come back to it. I'm not sure what that's all about but if the opportunity ever came up I might go for the whole look.

I am a Gay, white man and have been a wannabe for as long as I remember. I also have been a pretender, at time in public. Most of my escapades were at night with few people around, in my Quickie wheelchair or with forearm crutches. Because I am not thin—pretending to be an amputee is not possible as the doubling back of a limb makes too obvious of a bulge, so I go as a paraplegic. I have gone around the neighborhood at night and I also have visited the airport and post office while in the chair and/or using crutches. The car I have now does not permit carrying the wheelchair around easily and I've gotten heavier lately, so that crutch walking is very difficult. Because of this, most of my pretending has been at home. As for being a wannabe, my desires have changed radically over the years from being a simple BK(below-knee), to a quad. Primarily I focus on being a DAK(double above-knee) and would use a chair most of the time. If it were to happen tomorrow by accident, I would be O.K. with it, but as far as pursuing it independently—I don't think I'm ready. For some reason, I don't want anyone I know to be a part of my life when it happens. I want to start over. I don't want to have to lie to everyone I know about what happened and I don't want their pity.

Since many years I am attracted to female above-knee amputees. I have the desire to lose one of my legs so that every step has to be made with crutches. I think then I will feel satisfied. I would like to know in which manner an amputation is possible. Doctors don't amputate without medical reasons. How can I manage such a reason?

I'm almost 49, married, my wife does not know of this desire, and I am a pretender and sometimes I feel strongly about being a wannabe. I like to pretend being a DAK(double above-knee).

I desperately want a left above-knee amputation. I have wanted this since a child and I am now 35.

I am an amputee married to a devotee/wannabe. He spends 90% of his time in a wheelchair. We would like to know more on how he could fulfill his desire.

For as long as I can remember, the sight of a person with a missing limb attracted my attention. I have gone out of my way to follow an amputee, just to see how they deal with everyday matters. When I was in junior high school, I'd tie one or more limb(s) up so as to look like I was an amputee myself. One day, the next door neighbor knocked on the door to make sure I was all right. After that I made sure that the curtains were closed before I hopped around the house on one leg. In recent years, I have occasionally fantasized about being a DAK(double above-knee) amputee.

I have been an amputee wannabe for as long as I can remember. I thought I was different until recently when I found out that I am not alone in my desire to be an amputee. I have never had anyone that I could feel comfortable talking to about this and I have wanted so much to be able to talk to someone. As a child, I always had a fascination with amputated limbs and amputees. As I grew older, I began to realize it was more than just a fascination but an extreme desire to become an amputee myself. I could see myself enjoying any amputated limb or limbs that I might accidentally acquire. As I grew older, I knew that the only way I would ever really be happy and get the most out of my life was to voluntarily become an amputee. I think all amputations have a certain appeal whether they be arms or legs or arms and legs, double, triple or even quad. For the last few years I have wanted to give up both of my legs and have them both voluntarily amputated above the knees leaving me with very short, well formed stumps. Stumps that would give me countless hours of enjoyment. Stumps that would give me untold pleasure as I would fondle, caress and love them. Just writing about having both of my legs amputated gets me very excited and makes me even more determined to seek out a way to accomplish it. I have not been very successful in finding any sympathetic medical persons to help me out. I know they are out there somewhere. Has anyone ever found or made contact with a doctor who would actually do a voluntary amputation? I hope so. Again, it thrills me that I have actually made contact with other wannabes.

I have wanted to be a DAE(double above-elbow) for as long as I can remember. I want to find some help in completing this feat! Is anyone "out there" who could help me? I am really desperate! I have contemplated using the "train wheel" method, but have not figured out how to get to the hospital. I currently have no thumbs, as I cut them off in high school shop. I want this badly. Please help.

I have wanted to be an amputee for a number of years but have just recently discovered that I am not alone and there are actually people around that wouldn't find it distasteful! It seems that there are a number of "inmates in this asylum." I am a little different, it seems, from the "usual" female wannabe in that I want to lose my left arm by a complete and very clean disarticulation. I've made some noise, but I am a little shy about my desire and I'm not convinced that my wannabe issues fit well. I have, however, struck up some wonderful one-on-one E-mail chats with some of the members there.

As time grows near I am giddy with anticipation. After weeks of agonizing stress over this whole event I am now finally coming to terms with this. I have all of my plans finalized and everything is in place and planned out. The days of waiting are soon going to turn into hours then minutes and then seconds. Then in one fleeting second I will be what I was meant to be. I will see you on the other side....

I'm really new at being on a computer much less in communication with other wannabes. I'm not sure what a wannabe is but I think I may be one. I am removing myself from being a devotee, because it isn't what I'm looking for and it isn't really helping me explore my feelings. By the way, I'm 53, and female, if that matters.

I've wanted to be an amputee for most of my adult life. At the age of 37 I am not in a position to go forward to become a DAK(double above-knee), the most perfect form of physical being I have ever seen. I have had relationships with amputees but realize that this is no substitute for being one myself. Your help in getting to know others who think in the same way would be appreciated.

I am an arm amputee wannabe, more specifically, a bilateral below-elbow wannabe for many years, but have not yet taken the step to reach my desire. I would like to discuss the subject with other amputee wannabes or those who have achieved elective amputation in one way or another. I have rigged up bilateral prosthetic hooks which I use quite a bit around the house for long periods of time just to realize what would be in store for me, but also to convince myself that it really is what I want. Hopefully other members can help me.

I will always want a mid-forearm LBE(left below-elbow), but unless things change dramatically in my life, I will never have it. I am just fine with that! It was my decision to have two fingers amputated and as I have said before, these minor amputations have been more satisfying than I could ever have imagined. As it stands now I wouldn't change a thing!! If I had the opportunity in the future to realize the LBE amputation, you "betcha," I'd do it in a heartbeat!

I am a finger and toe amputee. Would like to be a leg amputee. Have always wanted to be. Finger and toe were fortunate accidents.

I have only just found out that I am not the only person in the world who is a wannabe. It has dominated my mind since I was very young. I had an aunt who was a RAK, and I used to watch her putting her stump in her prosthesis. It seemed quite natural. For as long as I can remember I have been attracted to female amputees. It is only a few days that I realize that there are so many others of us. I have thought about the "normal" things, I guess. Railway lines, self-injury necessitating amputation. What I would really like is to find a "friendly" surgeon who would understand! Payment would not be a problem. I am married to a wonderful woman. I am not sure how she would react to it, but obviously she would not realize that it had been "arranged."

6. Are the wannabes, devotees, or pretenders dangerous?

Recently, Robert Munro (1999) wrote, in the Nursing Times, that new amputees are being warned of devotees in this world. Devotees may be so driven by their inner impulse that their ethical and moral standards falter. There are cases where photographs of amputees were shared among fellow devotees without permission. Identifying information on some photographs have given devotees impetus to seek names, addresses, and phone numbers of the amputees in order to find them. On the other hand, some devotees are kind and want to help the amputee.

In general, all disabled people need to know that they are individuals; and that they have a right to love and be loved. It is wise to be open, yet aware and cautious of how and where they meet others, whether wannabe, devotee, pretender or anyone else. With the advance of the Internet, this advice is extended to disabled and able-bodied individuals.

7. How long has this syndrome been around?

Bruno (1997) writes, "Despite having been described for more than a century, there is no understanding of the origin of the attractions, desires and behaviors of devotees, pretenders and wannabes (DPWs)" (p. 1). Kraft-Ebing, (1953), reports that in Lydston's lecture on sexual perversions, a man had a relationship with a woman who was an amputee. Though over a century ago, this attraction is that of a devotee, and very likely the man was an acrotomophiliac (see Question # 26). We have no indication that he was an apotemnophiliac. However, London and Caprio (1950) report of a man who simulated an amputation of his leg and walked about, simulating an artificial leg or, "went out on crutches as a one-legged man" (p. 551). Here again, we do not have sufficient information, and all we definitely know is that this man is a pretender. He could or could not be technically a man who desires amputation of his leg, as some pretenders are not apotemnophiliacs (wannabes). As recent as October 7, 1999, Reuters News Service reported a 53-year-old Milwaukee man had devised a make-shift guillotine from information gleaned from the Internet, and severed his arm at the elbow. He told the authorities that he accidentally severed it working with tools at his home. The police investigated and found his arm in the refrigerator, wrapped in plastic. When confronted with the evidence, he admitted that he had built the device to amputate his arm and he refused to allow the surgeons to attempt reattaching the severed limb. He was doing fine physically, as reported in the paper, but the final line to the article stated, "Police said the man is undergoing psychological testing." As an apotemnophiliac, the man is doing fine; the authorities and medical professionals may not be doing as well.

The attitude is changing from 20 years ago. As this syndrome is explained to more and more people in society, they are open to hearing about it and are more willing to accept it. The medical profession has changed some, too. There are now cases where amputations have been performed on request; 20 years ago, when such help was sought, there was no discussion; the answer was automatically "NO!" Perhaps with the advancement of acceptance of the transsexual and of other groups formerly kept "in the closet," apotemnophilia and its implications will be better received. Hospitals and doctors have moved to help clients and have alleviated their trying to inflict self-injury. This is a time of change and possibilities.

8. When does the syndrome begin?

How this philia develops has not been verified. In personal cases which the authors have interviewed and cases which colleagues have reported, the apotemnophiliacs have had early childhood experiences with an amputee, which seem to have had input for triggering its development. All reported cases indicate that the desire is well implanted by puberty, and many clients report even earlier memories relating to the desire, commonly back to as early as 4 or 5 years of age.

9. What is the most difficult part of this syndrome?

It seems that, initially, the most difficult aspect of this syndrome is for individuals to accept who they are and admit that they suffer from this syndrome. The shame and guilt which encompasses these individuals, who find themselves having these feelings about disabilities, are enormous. It is, generally, not acceptable in our culture to be disabled, let alone have an unexplained desire and want for amputation or disability. These individuals feel they are disturbed and "sick." Frequently, they initially want to rid themselves of these thoughts and desires. But they soon find that it cannot exit from their psyches. Individuals report wanting to die, rather than come forward with this humiliating, embarrassing feeling that they cannot explain or understand. Being alone is very difficult. To some individuals this is such a burden of terror within, and even though they may have been in therapy for years, they have never spoken or told their therapists of the desire.

One has to remember, this is not a chosen or selected status. It is a given. It is much like one's sexuality. We do not select whether we will be heterosexual, homosexual, or bisexual. It is something one is. One does not select to have an eating disorder, or to be alcoholic. It is something within the individual psyche and soma. It is a burden to carry, yet it carries the great reward of feeling the identity and knowing what they should be. Just as transsexuals find themselves in a body that is not of their nature, apotemnophiliacs find themselves within a body that is not of their nature. As individuals who suffer from eating disorders find themselves within a body that is not of their desire or feeling, apotemnophiliacs find themselves captured and held within a body that is uncomfortable to live in.

To come forward and speak about what is happening within, thus opening oneself up to the taboos of culture and society, is risky. It is not easy. The statements and accusations made are debilitating and denigrating, and often lead those suffering to believe they should not be alive. Among apotemnophiliacs, agreement is not unanimous that information should be brought forward publicly. It is thought that it might destroy the chances of availability of elective surgery, and that society will continue to view apotemnophilia as a perversion, an illness to be corrected. Many apotemnophiliacs state that they do not care about the cause of the syndrome. They just want to fulfill the demand from within to live as they have to live.

10. Is this syndrome hereditary or learned?

It is not known if this syndrome is hereditary or learned. To date, some similar characteristics, though not necessarily always present, include lonely childhood experiences, unrelatedness in childhood days within the nuclear family, and early experience seeing or being around a disabled individual and noticing the love and affection placed on them. Current studies are trying to ascertain if there is a difference in the brain structure of apotemnophiliacs, compared to individuals who do not claim to have these desires.

11. Is this syndrome oriented mostly toward men?

Apotemnophilia is not just oriented to men. It seems to be found in both males and females. Statistics from the Ampulov (1999) Internet contact list, designed for wannabes, indicate that of 200 responses, men outnumber women 3 to 1. This was an Internet invitation study to submit information on wannabe status. This survey was not a randomly selected population, but this compilation of data is a remarkable contribution to the knowledge and understanding of this syndrome.

12. Is this syndrome dominated by a sexual orientation?

No sexual orientation seems to dominate. Heterosexuals, homosexuals, and bisexuals are included in reported cases. In addition, there are cases of transgendered individuals who also claim to be apotemnophiliacs, seeking sexual contact with their opposite sex.

13. Is apotemnophilia a fetish?

Apotemnophiliacs are not fetish oriented. A fetish is when an object is substituted for a human being as the primary relationship and becomes an object of divine devotion or blind affection. The amputation or its remnant is not a loved object used for sexual arousal. The primary relationship is not about the missing limb; rather, it is about living in the identity of an amputee, which the apotemnophiliacs feel is their natural body form. For the true apotemnophiliac, it is not about becoming disabled; it is, instead, about becoming able-bodied. Apotemnophiliacs are psychically oriented to living life on a daily basis as amputees, not because they think this is logical, or that they believe this will be easy, but because they know and feel that this would be living their natural way. Being four-limbed is not a normal status for them.

14. Can an individual control this urge?

This urge, this compulsion, is extremely difficult to stop or control. An individual must be willing to do so to succeed at all. It is like the wind, and can suddenly arrive full force upon the individual who can then be overwhelmed with desire. From all reported cases, it is so deeply ingrained within the apotemnophiliac that she/he cannot restrain or regulate its direction. In many reported cases, individuals have tried to rid themselves of its power, most frequently when they were younger, but the urge returns.

The power the syndrome has upon individual suffering is enormous. It has such impact that some human beings will go against cultural taboos and inflict personal mutilation to satisfy this call from within. It must, indeed, be an enormous oppression of their psyche and body, forcing individuals to fulfill the impelling desire. And all this is within persons who have been found by psychiatrists and psychologists not to be insane. C.G. Jung (1934/1969) speaks of this power as the power of an Archetype. We all know archetypes, for example, we know and have experienced the Mother archetype. When we speak of an archetype we are talking about the power within a mother that would demand/compel the woman to put her life in danger to protect and feed her children. This same driving force of energy, not of the Mother archetype, but of the dismemberment archetype, is what is within the apotemnophiliac. As a Mother cannot stop or control her instinctive archetypal urge to run into a burning house to save her children, so too, the apotemnophiliac cannot stop himself/herself from the dismemberment archetypal urge of seeking amputation.

15. Does therapy help?

As of this writing, there is no known therapy that has transformed the yearning and desire of this powerful urge for amputation. We have no evidence, but many professional therapists believe that behavioral therapy may help. While it does not seem to resolve the conflict, analytical therapy has helped individuals carry the burden without having to act aggressively against themselves. What is interesting is that several apotemnophiliacs who have been interviewed report that while they were in therapy, or, for those who are presently in therapy, they did not mention this amputation desire to their therapist. Reasons for not mentioning the desire ranged from shame, guilt, and embarrassment, to rationalizations that the therapist could not handle it. One apotemnophiliac stated that he did tell his therapist about his desire, but requested that the therapist never bring up the subject, and furthermore, never do anything therapeutically to squelch the longing. Additionally, this apotemnophiliac sought out a hypnotherapist. Hypnosis allowed him to live out his desire to feel and live life as an amputee.

16. Is there medicine that can help this syndrome?

Some medications exist which may or may not be helpful with this diagnosis. Clomipramine is reported to be used in some cases of body dysmorphism. Luvox, Paxil, Prozac, and Zoloft have been reportedly used for the obsessive-compulsive disorder, and for assistance with depression. However, as of this writing there are no known results reporting success, or of any treatment with drugs specifically for this syndrome.

17. Why is it so difficult to have surgery carried out?

The request for healthy limb amputation is, in general, anathema to a surgeon, as the first basic principle of the medical profession is "to do your patient no harm." To most surgeons, amputation of a normal limb is a complete abrogation of this principle—the amputation is a mutilating and disabling procedure. It is almost impossible to find a reputable surgeon prepared to carry out such a procedure.

Any surgeon approached with such a request must consider very carefully whether an amputation is in the client's best interest, and must consider whether the risks and long-term mobidity are a lesser complaint than the unresolved need to be an amputee. The surgeon becomes open to a number of ethical and legal pitfalls. Many members of the profession regard amputation of a normal limb unethical, regardless of the reasons. A surgeon who carried out such a procedure may, subsequently, be sued if the procedure does not result in the expected level of satisfaction or if there are any complications. The client must be fully informed of all possible complications and must sign a very carefully worded and witnessed consent.

At present, no hospitals seem prepared to allow these procedures (largely because of fear of adverse public reaction). The General Medical Council (responsible for ensuring the ethical standards of medical practice and the quality of its delivery) has little knowledge of the syndrome because there have been no published scientific studies. The Council will not offer any specific ethical advice on the subject and will only make a ruling if a complaint is raised (the Council is bound to investigate complaints).

18. Does surgery help?

There are four subtypes of individuals who seek amputation of a normal limb:

1.) The psychopathic self-mutilator. These individuals present with a history of self mutilation and will continue to require mutilating injuries or procedures. They will never be satisfied with a single amputation. Individuals who amputate multiple digits probably fall into this category.

2.) The dependence seeker. These individuals tend to require considerable support. They feel that if they become an amputee, it will result in an increased level of personal support and sympathy. Their situation could be resolved with non-surgical support.

3.) The acrotomophile wannabe. These individuals have a desire to be an amputee as a form of sexual arousal. They have variable ideas of which type of amputation they wish and the level and number of amputations varies from time to time. They have the desire to 'pretend' to be an amputee during sexual activity, but not during day to day activities. The 'pretending' may actually cause sexual arousal. Most, also, tend to be attracted to amputee partners (devotee) and may wish their partners also to "pretend." They are very unlikely to injure themselves to achieve their desire.

4.) The apotemnophile wannabe. These individuals have an irresistible and uncontrollable need to be an amputee. They have very definite, constant ideas of what type of amputation they wish. Few are 'devotees' or wish their partners to be amputees or to "pretend." These individuals are at true risk of self-injury to achieve their ends. Apotemnophiles are not about sexual gratification, but about the arousal of their identity as a fully functioning human being that they know they are.

Of the above, only the apotemnophile wannabe should be considered for therapeutic amputation. From a surgical perspective, the main concern is identifying the true wannabes and excluding the psychopathic, self-mutilators and the acrotomophile wannabes. A secondary issue is the individual who requests amputation of more than one limb. In a recent questionnaire on the Internet up to 50% of respondents indicated that they wished more than one limb amputated—some even wished four. This was, however, not a random sample and it is likely that many of the respondents were acrotomophile wannabes rather than apotemnophile wannabes. Logic dictates that if it is appropriate to amputate one limb, if an individual requests more than one limb amputated, it should be carried out. However, amputation of more than one limb is so mutilating that no surgeon is ever likely to comply.

Currently, we are aware of three known cases of elective surgery resulting in amputation of a lower limb. In all three cases, the individuals report great satisfaction and have become better integrated into their daily lives. These individuals have been observed to be more productive, happier, better related to their family and friends, and more confident in their world of work. Family members who know of the circumstances surrounding their voluntary elective surgery have expressed amazement at the change of attitude within the voluntary amputee, that they are better adjusted and easier to be around. In one case, a close family member of a voluntary amputee stated that if she had known that the amputation would have made this drastic a change in attitude and way of living for her sibling, she would have "chopped" the limb off for him earlier in his life.

In the six reported cases of self-mutilation resulting in surgical amputation of the desired limb, one individual died in his attempt to self-mutilate and one died following surgery; the four who survived the self-mutilating act ended with an amputation of the desired limb. These four individuals report great satisfaction, happiness, and delight with their end result. All four said: 1) that they regret that they did not do it earlier in life, and 2) that an enormous burden had been removed from their lives, and now they could get on with living. One voluntary leg amputee reported after his leg was amputated as a result of him shooting the lower half of the leg away, that "missing a leg is a minor inconvenience, compared to the burden of the desire," which had been hindering him from ". . . living life. I am much happier now--should have done it years ago."

19. Which limb is usually involved?

The limb to be amputated is usually specific to the individual who requests the elective surgery. There is a higher preference for leg amputation over arm amputation, yet both types of surgery are sought. Clients are certain of their choice of right or left leg, or right or left arm, and do not equivocate in their decision. The preference seems to lean toward amputation of the left leg.

Perhaps the choice has something to do with an early experience of seeing or being with a disabled individual, or with the client's own dexterity. One male apotemnophiliac stated that his first experience was with a left leg amputee at the age of 7, and that was his desired form of amputation. Another apotemnophiliac stated that he had early childhood physical problems with his right arm and had surgeries a few times and physical therapy over a period of years. This was his desired limb for amputation. Several apotemnophiliacs stated that they wanted the left limb amputated because it was their non-dominant extremity. The choice could also be related to Adler's (1938/1998) theory of "organ inferiority," where the limb that is most undeveloped in power and strength is the desired limb for sacrifice.

20. Is there a specific site for amputation?

For the apotemnophiliac, as stated above, there is, definitely, a particular limb to be removed, and, more specifically, a precise point for amputation. The definiteness of this is unparalleled compared to the rest of the known information about this syndrome. So much is indeterminate, obscure, and perplexing within this syndrome, holding dozens of unanswerable questions, but the specificity of the site for amputation is common within the range of apotemnophiliacs. As yet, there is no known reason or understanding for this exactness.

21. What can a person do about this syndrome?

Until recently, there was little to be done about this compulsion. Individuals suffered its possession, throwing themselves under trains, shooting themselves in the leg or arm with a shotgun, rifle, or handgun, or inflicting other injury. Today, as more is discovered about this diagnosis, therapy is available to help an individual carry its burden. But, while therapy does not seem to cure the syndrome, it has helped some individuals carry the conflict and adjust to its burden, so that individuals do not have to believe they are "crazy" or alone. The medical profession is now taking this syndrome more seriously, since it has seen so many trauma victims due to self wounding. There are a few hospitals and surgeons who will perform elective surgery for qualified patients who pass the screening standards of a psychological evaluation.

The syndrome can own an individual, to the extent of self-inflicted harm. It can have so much power that individuals can no longer have any control over their lives. It possesses them and they will do anything to answer its call, risking life, if necessary.

22. Where can one who has this need seek support?

Support groups can help. In the past, a small network of individuals would write to each other, talking and helping in as supportive a way as possible. This was difficult and very secretive, and many felt a tremendous burden of loneliness, guilt, and shame. Today the Internet has reachable groups, such as:
1. The Secret Garden:
    http://www.txh.com/secretgarden/
2. Paraamps: **http://www.paraamps.com**
3. Fascination: **http://super-hosting.com/fascination**
4. D-Links, the ultimate disability devotee links:
    http://d-links.com/indexa.htm#amp

5. Amputee World: **http://www.ampworld.de**

There are also hospitals and clinics that are open to help with counseling and testing to evaluate fitness and readiness for surgery. These sources can, also, be found on the Internet by communicating directly with an individual who has already been evaluated for, and is awaiting, such surgery.

23. What do non-elective amputees think of this syndrome?

Amputees who have lost a limb due to trauma or have had restorative surgery for a disfigured limb or other medical reason, have a broad range of responses toward this desire.

Some amputees view apotemnophiliacs with resentment and see those who desire amputation as "sick, disturbed, and crazy." They say it "is not easy living life as an amputee," and those who think it is, are uninformed. However, the apotemnophiliac does not seek an easy life as an amputee. Apotemnophiliacs believe that they are living in the "wrong body form," and though discomforts will be part of being an amputee, the resulting distress will be easier to live with, rather than to continue living life with the compulsion. One amputee, who intentionally shot his leg, which resulted in surgical removal above the wound, stated that "the inconvenience of being an amputee is easier to carry than the devouring compulsion which was killing me psychologically." To reiterate, this individual did not state that he thought it was an easy life as an amputee, but he was comparing his new life as an amputee to the suffering endured from the compulsion before surgery. An elderly lady of 77 years who had had a leg amputation for trauma at the age of 21 wrote, "Amputation is not so terrible. . . I can understand that mental torment is worse than amputation."

There are non-elective amputees who are supportive of those seeking elective surgery to become an amputee. They see this desire as helping amputees to be accepted in our society. They can understand the feeling of the apotemnophiliac and relate to it in an opposite way to their own dilemma. They see their suffering the loss of their limb in the same way as the apotemnophiliac's suffering having a limb that will not go away. Non-elective amputees suffer not being able to regain their lost limb; the apotemnophiliacs suffer from inability to rid themselves of the limb which will not go away. Both suffer and carry legitimate suffering.

Similar feelings arise from a sense of worthlessness and feeling "less than." Non-elective amputees may view themselves as impaired, and may feel "worthless and less than." Able-bodied apotemnophiliacs have similar feelings when viewing their body forms with all limbs, seeing themselves as "worthless and less than." Non-voluntary amputees cannot alter their new body form, missing a limb, but do use prostheses, go into rehabilitation, and strive for a return to a fulfilling wholeness. Voluntary amputees, as well, want to strive for resolution of their wholeness, and rid themselves of this "less than" feeling by seeking voluntary amputation, hoping to find fulfillment. In all the reported cases of voluntary amputation among apotemnophiacs we hear their regret that it was not done earlier in their lifetime. However, there are reported cases of dissatisfaction with voluntary amputation among acrotomophiliacs.

There are also non-elective amputees, who are either congenital amputees (born missing a limb), or trauma injured amputees who are apotemnophiliacs. One subject interviewed by the author was a double above-elbow arm congenital amputee who reported being an apotemnophiliac: he would become a pretender, having his partner tie his long stumps behind his back, so he could feel what it was like not having any arms. He also considered himself an acrotomophiliac (desiring sexual contact with other amputees), which was tremendously satisfying to him. He was seeking therapy for what looked like his affliction of being a double above-elbow arm amputee, but, rather, he sought counsel for the aloneness which he felt wanting to be with other amputees and to be without arms.

24. How do spouses and partners deal with this syndrome?

Responses to this question range from spouses and partners who have assisted their loved ones in damaging a limb to help achieve their desired amputation to those who are shocked to learn of the syndrome. Some spouses and partners have participated in pretender aspects, often fulfilling their loved ones and themselves. A few cases have been reported where spouses or partners could not let themselves be involved and could not understand the compulsion. Eventually, these relationships ended. More frequently than not, relationships cease because some wannabes, devotees, or pretenders cannot find it within themselves to share this desire with their significant other. They may live a lie, hold it within as "a secret," and then have to devise means and ways to live out the desire without their loved partner. Individuals with this syndrome need support and assistance to help them admit to themselves who and what they are, and that they need not be ashamed, embarrassed, humiliated, or demeaned. This honesty will help their relationship and if a split occurs, this alone will not be the reason.

25. Does publicity help or hurt the apotemnophiliacs' case?

This is a "catch-22" question: First, there is the medical community. Second, there is public reaction. Third, there are the apotemnophilacs. Fourth, there is the media.

First, many in the medical community are hesitant to step forward, for fear of being seen and known. Therefore, they do not help or deal seriously or constructively with those suffering from this diagnosis. Most professionals fear repercussions to themselves and their profession, and hide behind moral and ethical standards because they do not know what to do. In these cases, publicity does not help the medical community, nor does it help the apotemnophiliacs. However, there are a few pioneers in the medical profession willing to step forward and listen to their patients, and accompany them with their healing. They do not fear publicity, yet they do not seek it. In the cases where psychiatrists have assessed that the patient is fit for surgery, and where the surgeon has amputated the requested limb, there have only been successes. However, we must realize this number of patients is small. The fear is what will happen if surgery is performed on an individual who later has regrets. For this reason, pre-operative interviews and evaluations are stringent and lengthy. The request for surgery is not taken lightly, done hastily, or without extensive assessment.

Second, public reaction is much different than what was expected. Usually, when the public learns that apotemnophiliacs feel trapped physically and psychically in a body that is not their body form and that they know and feel their natural state of living life would be as an amputee, the public generally accepts the concept of amputation. Publicity is good for both groups, as it is further education toward understanding of an unknown phenomenon. When the public knows that this syndrome involves extensive testing, assessment, and evaluation, we then find more acceptance of the apotemnophiliacs' request. There are certain religious and conservative factions, both in the medical community and the public, who believe apotemnophiliacs **should** be protected from themselves. They believe that others cannot have a different psychology. It is difficult for them to conceive of others thinking and acting differently from their norm. However, this is not the vast majority of the general public who are supportive of requested surgery.

Third, apotemnophiliacs who have been helped with surgery seem to construct a new way of living, and have little or no interest in being aligned with the wannabe world again. They settle into active living with family and work. They are happy, productive, and no longer involved in this philia world. Their family members report a dramatic change in their co-operation and joy in living life, and are pleased with those changes. Apotemnophiliacs who have been helped with surgery show little interest in publicity of this phenomenon and generally do not want to be involved; they primarily just want to get on with their lives.

Among apotemnophiliacs seeking surgery, there is a greatly mixed review toward publicity of this philia. Some see publicity as education, and that the culture and public need to be informed, to accept and reach out to help those suffering from this diagnosis. Others see publicity as an act of desperation from their fellow wannabes who are willing to do anything to get surgery.

Fourth, the media world seems to have two intertwined agendas: money making and education. The media world exists and operates to reach out to the public. To reach out to the collective, the media must have some content to share. This philia is uncommon, exotic, maybe even bizarre. It surely carries with it an attention "getter" for the curious and, yet, it may make some people feel uncomfortable. There is definitely content to share with the public. For the media, this is a saleable topic to discuss and publicize, on the radio, television, or in newspapers or magazines. This topic gets attention and sells, providing a monetary bottom line very important to many in the media. The monetary agenda looks dirty/malicious, the education agenda looks honorable.

26. Is acrotomophilia the same as apotemnophilia?

No. Acrotomophilia describes a person who is sexually stimulated with the theme or idea of having sex with a person who is disabled. Most frequently it is with an amputee, but does include the paraplegic or others with another disability. The common term is "devotee." The acrotomophiliac can see the body form of the disabled as "the loved object," and is often caught by the fetish.

Bruno (1977) cites Nattress' (1996) unpublished doctoral dissertation that acrotomophiles do have low ratings on "social interest, emotional stability and personal relations" (p. 2).

> The low scores were referred to by Nattress as 'problematic behavior tendencies.' Such

tendencies have become a concern of people with disabilities since devotees do demonstrate problematic behaviors, ranging from collecting names, addresses, and phone numbers of disabled persons to obsessive and intrusive phone calls, letters, and e-mail to persons with disabilities, attending and sometimes organizing disability-related events, lurking in public places to watch, taking covert pictures of, talking to and touching disabled persons, and even engaging in predatory stalking. (1,3,19) For example, over 85% of Nattress' sample agreed with the statement, 'If I see a female amputee at a shopping mall I will follow her,' and over 57% agreed that, 'If I see a female amputee in a store I will try to talk to her.' (p. 2)

According to Dixon (1983), most acrotomophiliacs interested in amputees are college-educated, professional, white males who have had a sexual interest in amputees since puberty. Over half of the acrotomophiliacs noted themselves as pretenders and three-quarters of them had fantasies of being an amputee, thus qualifying them as wannabes.

Some disabled individuals strongly dislike acrotomophiles who find them sexually desirable because of their disability, while other disabled individuals are open to the attention and desire. Most disabled individuals agree that they do not want to be desired just for their disability, but for who they are as a person. However, in reported cases where marriage has resulted between an acrotomophiliac and a disabled individual, eventually the acrotomophiliac states that the disability is not the driving force after the initial relatedness begins, but the personality and humanness of the disabled person prevails in the marriage or relationship.

27. What is mutilation, and how is it related?

Mutilation as defined in the <u>American Heritage Dictionary</u> (1996), is "rendering imperfection onto the body by damaging or excising a part.... Latin *mutilare*, cut off, from *mutilus,* maimed." Looked at psychically, an individual may be cut off and/or maimed outwardly and inwardly. Furthermore, mutilation can be seen psychologically as a call for psychic change. Peters (1994) notes in his article, "Rites of Passage and the Borderline Syndrome," that all mutilation is done "to aid the process of passage" (p. 6). He reports that Eliade considers

> the existential state of consciousness created during initiations to be one of 'dread,' 'awe,' and of a 'belief in impending death.' Everything is done to cause a 'disintegration of the personality.' In other words, there is a nonordinary state of consciousness created, typically through fasting, ingesting of psychoactive drugs, and physical deprivations and mutilations, all to aid the process of passage; disintegration, transformation, and psychosocial reintegration. (p. 6)

Mutilation, as a process, is ritualized in hair pulling (trichotillomania), nail biting, scarification, drug abuse, and eating disorders. Ross and McKay (1979) disclose two classifications for self mutilation: 1) Direct Self-Injurious Behaviors, which are immediate and certain, such as cutting, biting, severing, burning, ingesting, hitting, or constricting, and 2) Indirect Self-Injurious Behaviors, which are long term and uncertain, such as obesity, alcohol abuse, smoking, drug abuse, or refusing medical treatment. This ordering system helps create a beginning understanding of the reported style of self-mutilation. The categories are not mutually exclusive and there is overlap.

Mutilating behavior often overwhelms individuals, as if "called," contained, even possessed to such an extent that they cannot pull themselves away from its ritualistic psychic suction.

The wannabe, pretender, and devotee have this same psychic suction. In one culture, this act can be seen as negative; yet, in another culture the same act can be seen as a positive developmental stage of growth.

28. Are therapists ready for this syndrome?

(Gregg M. Furth, Ph.D., reports his experience as a professional therapist.)

Many apotemnophiles have told me that they fear reporting this syndrome to their therapists. It is unbelievable to me, but some clients in therapy for several years have never discussed this subject with their therapist. These clients tell me that they believe their therapists will not comprehend this syndrome and believe their therapists will not know how to handle it. Other clients with this syndrome report that the initial response of their therapists will be to rid them of the desire, rather than to listen to or understand them. Therefore, clients do not confide in their therapists out of fear of rejection and being misunderstood.

I originally thought these clients were being defensive and that they were embarrassed and ashamed to tell their therapists of their desires. At one point, I did not accept that the therapists would be unable to handle this information. However, when I was asked to speak to a Jungian group in Portland, Oregon, on a unrelated topic, it seems that a professional senior analyst in Palo Alto, California, who had learned of this syndrome and its consequences from newspaper reports I was involved in, reported what he heard to the Oregon group. This group became frightened to allow me to lecture. I contacted this Jungian analyst to inquire into the nature of his fear. He told me that years ago, in college, a communist speaker at his school "terrified" the audience. He told me of his fear that the audiences today could not handle this information about this syndrome, if by chance someone asked a question about it. This senior analyst certainly proves that senior does not necessarily imply having wisdom, experience and knowledge. His fear seemed to be an unresolved inner conflict which he was projecting onto others. This colleague told me that when he first heard my voice on the telephone, he was nervous and upset, but after our discussion which included a brief education on this syndrome, he reported that he calmed down and was more settled within. This reaffirms what clients have reported to me about therapists being opinionated and unable to hear, understand, and help with this syndrome.

In another situation, I was to lecture, again, on a different topic to a Jungian group in Washington, D.C. and this lecture/workshop was also cancelled. The psychiatrist from this group stated that she had never heard of nor met any patients with this syndrome. Individuation was not of concern to her. She reported that she did not deny the syndrome, but she was determined that all clients should be treated in her style of therapy to "become normal," and would not accept that any apotemnophile could be supported for surgery, regardless of recommendations or the client's life need. She also added that there should be no transgender surgery. These reported examples from "professional colleagues," tell me that members of my profession are very likely to be scared and unsure of what to do with a client living with this syndrome. I now believe my clients and those who have phoned to me for help concerning this syndrome when they speak of their therapists' denial and fear.

As stated in Chapter 1, we urge all health care providers to:

1. understand that everyone has his or her individual psychology, and that others do not necessarily have the same psychology as the provider,
2. dare to set aside personal prejudices, endeavor to be open, be willing to listen to another's reality, regardless of how it may differ, and
3. understand that the primary goal is for respect, that this syndrome is a real-life occurrence for many individuals, and that they suffer from it.

If health care providers can agree to these three premises, progress may be made for all concerned. Consciousness, education, acceptance, understanding, respect, and cordiality are sought. We are not asking that health care providers recommend clients for surgery, we are asking health care providers to hear and to help clients become conscious and to allow for the process of Individuation to occur.

We continue, as professionals, to urge clients to tell their therapists everything truthfully. Clients should seek assistance from other professionals if their therapists do not understand or are unable to help them with this syndrome. We continue to recommend that clients inform their therapists about this syndrome and deal with the issue of their shame and embarrassment and their fear of being rejected, misunderstood, criticized and devalued by their therapist. We also urge clients to avoid the hazardous practice of attempting to injure themselves, as an injury sufficient to require major amputation may well be fatal. With this in mind, we continue to support, where necessary, that some apotemnophiles are good candidates for surgery, as a last resort, after comprehensive assessment, when all other remedies have failed.

CHAPTER V
FUTURE RECOMMENDATIONS

Possibilities for recommendations range from establishing surgical procedures for the requested amputation to intensive therapeutic programs for rehabilitation. After carefully studying and speaking with clients who classify themselves as apotemnophiliacs, wannabes, devotees, or pretenders; the following suggestions are offered:

- Make available a behavioral therapeutic program for apotemnophiliacs, wannabes, pretenders, or devotees.
- Establish and monitor a medication program for those who want to attempt drug rehabilitation.
- Further develop the Internet for supplying information and support groups to apotemnophiliacs and amputees. A support network like this is not a new idea. Recovering alcoholics have Alcoholics Anonymous, recovering gamblers have Gamblers' Anonymous, and there are many such groups for different problem areas today.
- Form more groups via the Internet, like Fascination, established by Betty Haglund, in Chicago. These groups could serve heterosexuals, homosexuals, and bisexuals. Additionally, they could have annual conventions, open not only to devotees but wannabes and pretenders, as well.
- Provide more research to detect the scope and depth of this desire. Therapists are needed to observe and aid in the consciousness of the desire, putting their biases aside. Openness and acceptance are needed by therapists who dare to deal with this phenomenon.
- Provide more research into the etiology of this disorder, as well as research regarding healing methods.
- Work to enlighten those professionals who are strongly opinionated against this syndrome. Prejudices by therapists are enormous and clients are dubious about trusting and working with opinionated and dictatorial counselors. When

the medical profession is open to discussing this syndrome, there will be hope for recognition and resolution. This will have an enormous effect on those diagnosed with this condition.
- Establish networking for the development of wannabe limb donation to transplant teams for limb replacement in research hospitals.
- Maintain total confidentiality.
- Suggestions and recommendations for interviewing potential clients for surgery or therapy regarding this desire are:
    --gather background data, history, duration of desire, relatedness to family and significant other, and how this could be inter-related in a compensatory/complementary manner.
    --require a physical and emphasize not just the limb desired to be removed, but the entire body, so it can support the individual if such surgery is carried out.
    --recommend and assess a minimum one year simulation where the client requesting surgery lives the closest possible parallel to the disability they desire.
- Establish a structured program of assessment for surgery with a clear list of diagnostic criteria.
- Produce information documents on the condition, the surgical procedure, and complications and rehabilitation.
- All patients should be entered into clinical studies. All patients, already treated by any form of behavioral modification and especially those treated by surgery, should receive long term psychological monitoring.
- Develop a structured consent to be completed before surgery.
- Provide medically advised surgery as a viable option to clients who qualify via assessments and evaluations made by a team of three professionals. The referrals should come from licensed professionals, such as psychotherapists, psychologists, psychiatrists, analysts, or social workers.

- A study of apotemnophiles who have achieved amputation needs to be made to assess the long term results of amputation.
- Establish a committee within a recognizable professional organization, such as The American Psychological Association or The American Psychiatric Association, to develop and implement alternative suggestions and courses of action in dealing with this syndrome.
- Define, differentiate, and categorize apotemnophilia as a legitimate diagnostic syndrome in the <u>Diagnostic and Statistical Manual</u>. For example, a citing could read:

> <u>Body Identity Disorder</u>[2]
> Diagnostic features:
> > There are two components of Body Identity Disorder, both of which must be present to make the diagnosis. There must be evidence of a strong and persistent disability identification, which is the desire to be, or the insistence that one is, internally, disabled (Criterion A). The disability identification must not merely be a desire for any perceived cultural advantages of living with a disability. There must also be evidence of persistent discomfort about living as an able-bodied person, or a sense of inappropriateness in that same role (Criterion B). The diagnosis is not made if the condition is better explained by another medical or psychiatric diagnosis (Criterion C). To make the diagnosis, there must be evidence of clinically significant distress or

---

[2] As noted earlier, the name Apotemnophilia needs to be changed and updated. Body Identity Disorder is a suggested title for this syndrome as is the accompanying description.

impairment in social, occupational, or other important areas of functioning (Criterion D).

This identification is manifested by a marked preoccupation with activities associated with living as a person with a disability. Depending on the particular disability identified with, the person may attempt to simulate amputation by "binding" one or more limbs in a bent position, or attempt to simulate paralysis by using household objects to brace limb(s), leaving the limb(s) in question temporarily unable to function normally. There may also be a strong fascination with assistive devices used by people with disabilities (ex. wheelchairs, crutches, braces, prosthetics, etc.).

Many adults with this disorder are preoccupied with a desire to live as a disabled person – either by using various assistive devices to simulate disability, or by taking drastic steps to cause an accident which might lead to the acquisition of the desired disability. People who use various assistive devices to voluntarily limit their own mobility are often referred to as "pretenders." Some people pretend only rarely, in the privacy of their own homes, and some pretend occasionally in public. Some people find that their desires are best managed by living their entire public life as if they had a disability. People who engage in "pretending" almost invariably report a feeling of wholeness that accompanies their simulation and an absence of that feeling when living as an able-bodied person. Desperation can lead people with this disorder to the point of endangering their lives in attempting to become disabled. Examples include people who have cut limbs off with chainsaws, positioned their bodies on train tracks in an attempt to lose a limb or multiple limbs, caused irreparable damage to limbs with firearms, caused traffic accidents, or jumped from roofs in an attempt to cause a spinal cord injury (contributed by a wannabe who is also a therapist, using the DSM IV description of Gender Identity Disorder as a template. E-mail for this person can be sent to: WannabeIssues@aol.com).

REFERENCES

Adler, A. (1998). <u>Social interest</u>. Boston: Oneworld Publications.

American Psychiatric Association. (1994). <u>Diagnostic and statistical manual of mental disorders</u> (4th ed.). Washington, DC: Author.

Ampulov (1999). Available: http://www.ampulove.com

Bruno, R. (1997). Devotees, pretenders and wannabes: Two cases of factitious disability disorder. <u>Journal of Sexuality and Disability, 15</u>, 243-260.

Campbell, J. (1973). <u>The hero with a thousand faces</u>. Princeton, NJ: Bollingen Series XVII.

Dixon, D. (1983). An erotic attraction to amputees. <u>Sexuality and Disability 6</u>, 3-19.

Ebin, V. (1979). <u>The body decorated</u>. London: Thames & Hudson.

Edinger, E.F. (1972). <u>Ego & archetype—Individuation and the religious function of the psyche</u>. Boston: Shambhala.

Eliade, M. (1974). <u>Shamanism: Archaic techniques of ectasy</u>. Princeton, NJ: Bollingen Series LXXVI.

Eliade, M. (1987). <u>The encyclopedia of religion</u>. New York: Macmillan.

Elder, G.R. (1996). <u>An encyclopedia of archetypal symbolism, Vol. 2, The body</u>. Boston: Shambhala.

Estes, C.P. (1992). <u>Women who run with the wolves: Myths and stories of the wild woman archetype</u>. New York: Ballantine Books.

Everaerd, W. (1983). A case of apotemnophilia: A handicap as sexual preference. <u>American Journal of Psychotherapy, 37</u> (2), 285-293.

Favazza, A.R. (1996). <u>Bodies under siege: Self-mutilation and body modification in culture and psychiatry</u>. Baltimore: The Johns Hopkins University Press.

Freud, S. (1964). Anxiety and instinctual. In J. Strachey (Ed. and Trans.), <u>The standard edition of the complete psychological works of Sigmund Freud</u> (Vol. 22, pp. 81-111). London: The Hogarth Press and The Institute of Psycho-Analysis. (Original work published (1933 [1932])

Gould, G. & Pyle, W. (1956). <u>Anomalies and curiosities of medicine</u>. New York: Bell.

Harper, M.J. (1996). <u>And how shall I be me? An exploration of childhood self-mutilation</u>. Unpublished Master's thesis. Pacifica Graduate Institute, Carpinteria, CA.

Herman, J. (1992). <u>Trauma and recovery: The aftermath of violence—from domestic abuse to political terror</u>. New York: Basic Books.

Jung, C.G. (1966). Two essays on analytical psychology. In R.F.C. Hull (Trans.), <u>The collected works of C.G. Jung</u> (Vol. 7). Princeton, NJ: Princeton University Press. (Original work published in 1917)

Jung, C.G. (1969). The structure and dynamics of the psyche. In R.F.C. Hull (Trans.), <u>The collected works of C.G. Jung</u> (Vol. 8). Princeton, NJ: Princeton University Press. (Original work published in 1934)

Jung, C.G. (1971). Psychological Types. In R.F.C. Hull (Trans.), <u>The collected works of C.G. Jung</u> (Vol. 6). Princeton, NJ: Princeton University Press. (Original work published in 1921)

Jung, C.G., (1968). Psychology and alchemy. In R.F.C. Hull (Trans.), <u>The collected works of C.G. Jung</u> (Vol. 12). Princeton, NJ: Princeton University Press. (Original work published in 1953)

Jung, C.G. (1969). Psychology and religion: West and east. In R.F.C. Hull (Trans.), <u>The collected works of C.G. Jung</u> (Vol. 11). Princeton, NJ: Princeton University Press. (Original work published in 1937)

Jung, C.G. (1969). Psychology and religion: West and east. In R.F.C. Hull (Trans.), <u>The collected works of C.G. Jung</u> (Vol. 11). Princeton, NJ: Princeton University Press. (Original work published in 1958)

Kirk, S. (1995). What the gender community needs from the medical community. <u>The TV/TS Tapestry, 70,</u> 9-10.

Kraft-Ebing, R. von (1953). <u>Psychopathia Sexualis</u>. New York: Pioneer. (Original work published in 1906)

Kubler-Ross, M.D., E. (1969). <u>On death and dying</u>. New York: Macmillan.

Lincoln, B. (1981). <u>Emerging from the chrysalis: Studies in rituals of women's initiation</u>. Cambridge, MA: Harvard University Press.

London, L. & Caprio, F. (1950). <u>Sexual deviations</u>. Washington, D.C.: The Linacre Press.

Love, B. (1995). Encyclopedia of unusual sex practices. London: Abacus.

MacKenzie, G.O. (1994). Transgender nation. Bowling Green, OH: Bowling Green University Popular Press.

Metsker, K. (1989). Transsexuals and their parents. The TV/TS Tapestry, 53, 23-26.

Miller, D. (1994). Women who hurt themselves: A book of hope and understanding. New York: Basic Books.

Soukhanov, A. H. (Ed.) (1996). American heritage dictionary of the English language. Boston, MA: Houghton Mifflin.

Money, J., Jobaris, R. & Furth, G. (1977). Apotemnophilia: Two cases of self-demand amputation as a paraphilia. The Journal of Sex Research, 13 (2), 115-125.

Munro, R. (1999). When amputation is the only option. Nursing Times, 95 (40), 26-30.

Neuman, E. (1954). The origins and history of consciousness. New York: Pantheon.

Peters, L.G. (1994). Rites of passage and the borderline syndrome: Perspective in transpersonal anthropology. Anthropology of Consciousness, 5 (1), 1-15.

Reuters News Service (1999, Oct. 7), Chicago News Bureau.

Ross, R.R. & McKay, H.B. (1979). Self-mutilation. Lexington, MA: Lexington Books, D.C. Heath.

Virel, A. (1980). Ritual and seduction: The human body as art. London: New English Library.

Walsh, B. & Rosen, P. (1988). <u>Self-mutilation: Theory, research and treatment</u>. New York: The Guilford Press.

ABOUT THE AUTHORS

Robert Smith, the son of a surgeon, was born in Scotland and gained his medical degree at the University of Edinburgh in 1970. He trained in general surgery in several hospitals in Edinburgh and became a Fellow of the Royal College of Surgeons of Edinburgh in 1974. After several years of clinical research he qualified Ch.M. of Edinburgh University. He worked as a research fellow and honorary senior resident at McMaster University, Hamilton, Ontario for a year before returning to the UK in 1980. He became a Consultant in General and Vascular Surgery in Falkirk and District Royal Infirmary in 1982.

His research interests are in vascular surgery and surgical education, and he has lectured and examined in surgery in many countries around the world. He is a keen surgical teacher and his clinical interests include vascular and thoracic surgery, and the early rehabilitation of amputees.

Gregg M. Furth has a Ph.D. from Ohio State University with concentration on investigation of drawings as a viable aid in counseling. He has a Master's degree in counseling psychology and has spent the last 30 years working with emotionally disturbed and terminally ill children and adults. Furth has conducted hundreds of workshops worldwide on such topics as Hospice training; Death, Dying and Bereavement; Picture Interpretation; Basics of Analytical Psychology; The Word Association Experiment; Symbols in Healing; Anger, Guilt and Projection; Active Imagination; Therapeutic Art Methods Training; and The Great Mother. His research led to the original writing on the topic of Apotemnophilia in 1977 with J. Money and R. Jobaris. He is a contributing author of *Living With Death and Dying* by Elisabeth Kübler-Ross. He has written *The Secret World of Drawings: Healing Through Art, A Jungian Approach,* which is now published in six languages. He is a graduate of the C.G. Jung Institute, Zurich, and is presently practicing in New York City.

Printed in the United Kingdom
by Lightning Source UK Ltd.
2226